T0277592

PRAISE FOR

Don't Settle

"In *Don't Settle: A Pick-Your-Path Guide to Intentional Work*, George Appling's perspective provides the tactics unique to tackling the significant and personal challenge of what to do with your work life. As George suggests, 'It's about intentionally choosing the relationship between your work and your passion. If I can help you align how you make a living with something that you're passionate about, it's going to lead to an increase in joy for you.' Who doesn't want that?"

—SAM REESE, CEO, Vistage Worldwide, Inc.

"George Appling is the fusion of childlike joy, analytical genius, and love of others, and he has used those traits to build himself a wonderful life. Here Appling lays out a path toward building your own wonderful life, based on your own values and joys. This path is built on tactics and techniques derived both from his own experience and leading scientific understanding and is refined with George's particular skill at figuring out what works in any situation. If you are ready to do the work, this book will be a powerful tool."

—CHAD ELLIS, CEO, Boda Borg; Harvard Business School Baker Scholar

"I've had the distinct pleasure of working with George for over thirty years, and he's been making a difference in whatever he does. He has always applied both creativity and structure to his work, resulting in highly insightful and pragmatic ways of thinking and frameworks that deliver results. I'm excited to see the concepts and frameworks in *Don't Settle* help young people in their journeys forward."

—**KENNY KURTZMAN,** managing director and senior partner, Boston Consulting Group

Don't Settle

Don't Settle

A PICK-YOUR-PATH GUIDE TO INTENTIONAL WORK

GEORGE APPLING

GREENLEAF
BOOK GROUP PRESS

This publication is designed to provide accurate and authoritative information in regard to the subject matter covered. It is sold with the understanding that the publisher and author are not engaged in rendering legal, accounting, or other professional services. Nothing herein shall create an attorney-client relationship, and nothing herein shall constitute legal advice or a solicitation to offer legal advice. If legal advice or other expert assistance is required, the services of a competent professional should be sought.

Published by Greenleaf Book Group Press
Austin, Texas
www.gbgpress.com

Copyright © 2024 George Appling

All rights reserved.

Thank you for purchasing an authorized edition of this book and for complying with copyright law. No part of this book may be reproduced, stored in a retrieval system, or transmitted by any means, electronic, mechanical, photocopying, recording, or otherwise, without written permission from the copyright holder.

Distributed by Greenleaf Book Group

For ordering information or special discounts for bulk purchases, please contact Greenleaf Book Group at PO Box 91869, Austin, TX 78709, 512.891.6100.

Design and composition by Greenleaf Book Group
Cover design by Greenleaf Book Group
Cover Images: MicroOne/shutterstock.com; Kostiantyn/stock.adobe.com.
Cover art dedicated to the Sherwood Forest Faire archery community and Trad Tour Archery.

Publisher's Cataloging-in-Publication data is available.

Print ISBN: 979-8-88645-187-0

eBook ISBN: 979-8-88645-188-7

To offset the number of trees consumed in the printing of our books, Greenleaf donates a portion of the proceeds from each printing to the Arbor Day Foundation. Greenleaf Book Group has replaced over 50,000 trees since 2007.

Printed in the United States of America on acid-free paper

24 25 26 27 28 29 30 31   10 9 8 7 6 5 4 3 2 1

First Edition

Only 20 percent of young people are lucky enough to know what they want to do with their lives.[1]

This book is dedicated to anyone in the 80 percent ready to change that stat.

Contents

Introduction

On a warm November weekend not too long ago, I traveled more than a hundred miles to meet an old friend of mine. We greeted each other outside the venue of a workshop we were both attending, and I commented on a family relationship: I'd been engaged to Nox's sister some time ago but had changed my mind. He said something insulting, and I called him on it. He drew his sword and ran at me.

It was a longsword, a surprisingly nimble two-handed weapon more than three feet in length. I dropped into a fighting stance, preparing to meet his blade with my own. They crashed together with a familiar metallic ring that always made me smile. Nox took a step back, and I followed with a downstroke. He deflected. I swung again, stepping closer, aiming for his chest. He caught the blow with his sword at right angles to mine. For a moment, we were locked together, evenly matched. He rallied and threw me off. I backed up a few paces, but we both knew how it would end—with him on his knees, my sword at his throat, and our longsword stage combat certification renewed. No, I hadn't *really* been engaged to his sister. That was just the theatrical story we were telling. It was a good day.

I have a lot of good days. I've been happily partnered for twenty-seven years as of 2023, have three great kids, and no boss. My family is financially secure, and I spend my time working hard doing things I love. I own a medieval theme park, run a summer camp, and advise CEOs as a Vistage chair. I'm the most fulfilled and joyful person I know.

Part of this is temperament: I've always been a high-energy, optimistic person. Some of it is luck: I was born male and white with loving parents living in a first-world democracy, and I had some terrific high school teachers. But this isn't a book about happiness. There are a lot of high-energy white guys with good parents who aren't half as fulfilled by their lives as I am by mine. And *that* has to do with some discoveries and choices I've made.

By the time I was seventeen, I'd learned the value of being—and staying—physically fit. It just feels better to live inside a strong and healthy body. Exercise reduces stress, helps you sleep, makes you look good, improves thinking, and prevents disease. In fact, vigorous physical activity drives down your chances of heart disease and cancer (the top two killers in the USA) and your chances of being diagnosed with anxiety and depression.[1]

This doesn't have to mean running miles or lifting weights. You can experiment until you find a form of exercise that you enjoy enough to stick with it. If being on the water makes you feel great, try rowing. If you love to dance, consider something like Zumba. Even walking with purpose (somewhere between powerwalking and strolling) can get your heart up to 60 percent of its maximum rate if you cover two miles in fewer than forty minutes.

PHYSICAL FITNESS PREVENTS ROUGHLY EVERYTHING BAD.

But this isn't a book about physical fitness. It's a toolkit and framework you can use to intentionally choose the relationship between your passion and your work because there's a mental correlate to physical fitness: being intentional.

Being intentional is a kind of superpower. If you're in a bad mood, there are a few deliberate steps you can take that are almost guaranteed to cheer you up—write down three things you're grateful for, exercise, take a walk outside, or call a loved one. If you're not happy with your life, you can start making specific plans to create one you'll love. Hell, if you're out of shape, get intentional about becoming physically fit. Almost every good thing I have in my life has the same origin story. I first identified something I wanted. Then I did what I needed to do to get it.

Everything you do all day, every day is a choice—what you eat, how you spend your time, and who you spend it with. Choosing not to be intentional means letting other people, or life's default settings, make your choices *for* you. The question, of course, is: *How?*

To answer that (for now), here's an old joke:

Question: How do you get to Carnegie Hall?
Answer: Practice.

Practice is how you get anywhere and accomplish anything. And everything is practice. What have you done
regularly to get where you are right now? What did you
practice doing today? Right now, you're practicing reading.
And because you're reading a book about being intentional,
you're also practicing improving yourself—which means you're
already ahead of everyone who's practicing watching TV.
And here's where we get tactical. We're going to practice
practicing.

Throughout this book, I'm going to provide opportunities
for you to engage more deeply with the material. I believe that
just reading it will help you, but I'm
completely convinced that if you do
the tactical components, it will make
a significant, positive difference in
your life. So get yourself a pen and
get ready. We're not even waiting
for Chapter 1 to practice getting
into action.

**BEING
INTENTIONAL
MEANS
CONSCIOUSLY
OWNING YOUR
CHOICES.**

Take Action on Becoming More Intentional

Since being intentional is the mental equivalent of being
physically fit, we'll start by getting a baseline. If I wanted to
assess your physical fitness, I could measure your body fat

percentage and blood pressure or see how far you can sprint before you drop or how many sit-ups you can do.

Measure your intentional fortitude: Look back over the last two years and identify what, if any, quantifiable goals[*] you set for yourself in the categories found in the following table.

- List them.

- Put a star by the ones you've achieved.

	Quantifiable Goal Set
Education	
Relationships	
Career	
Financial	
Experience	
Fitness	

Score yourself: Award one point for each goal you listed and another point for every star.

- 10+ points = You're intentional

- 5–10 points = You can do it!

- <5 points = You *really* need this book!

---

[*] A quantifiable goal is one that doesn't allow for any ambiguity. This is the difference between a vague goal such as "exercise more" and the more quantifiable "go to the gym four times a week every week for the next three months."

Bonus points: Complete the following table for your future goals.

	Quantifiable Goal	Timeframe (by when and for how long?)	Achievable First Step	Next Step after That
Education				
Fitness				
Relationships				
Career				
Financial				
Experience				

The more intentional you are, the more choices you can make. This book is about how to make one of the most significant choices any of us gets to make: what to do with your work life. I believe that if you can align what you're passionate about with a way of making a living, it will lead to an increase in joy. Happily, I probably have less work to do to convince you of this idea than I would have with any previous generation. Maybe it comes from having seen too many adults drag themselves through the week, but almost half of Gen Z is already on board, identifying their top indicator of success as having a career they're passionate about.[2] This is fantastic. The only difference I'm going to suggest is that alignment doesn't have to mean overlap. There are a variety of different ways the thing or things you're passionate about can intersect and interact with how you support yourself financially.

I've read a host of books on the topics of life purpose and career planning and found most to be long on inspiration and short on tactics. To me, it feels a bit like being told the best way to get to somebody's house is by riding a horse or flying a plane. Even assuming you can get good instruction on horse riding or plane flying, if you don't have the street address, you're going to have trouble. So aside from the fact that I've read a lot on the matter (because maybe you have too), why should you listen to me?

YOU MUST BE INTENTIONAL ABOUT THE RELATIONSHIP BETWEEN YOUR PASSIONS AND YOUR PROFESSIONAL PATH.

Hi, I'm George

I have two bachelor's degrees, one in business and the other in government, from Texas A&M University, where, at graduation, I ranked first in both the College of Business and the College of Liberal Arts. I also have two master's degrees, again in business and government, from Harvard. I've worked in Germany, England, Australia, Russia, China, and all over the US, and have professional experience in business, government, the arts, and the nonprofit world. I've been a consultant, held C-suite roles, and worked with everything from Fortune 500 companies to medium-sized operations to small local ones. And I can throw a spear from the back of a running horse with deadly accuracy.

I'm also a Vistage chair,[†] own part of a mead-making company, and run a ren faire and a summer camp. I also run a nonprofit program doing equine therapy for first responders, veterans, and active-duty military (motto: "Keep Calm and Do Epic Stuff"). But perhaps my two most significant qualifications for being a guy you listen to about what to do with your life are these: I love the life I've made for myself, and I really did create it intentionally.

There are already several excellent books written by people with advanced degrees about being intentional in your life plan. Perhaps the best is *Designing Your Life* by Bill Burnett and Dave Evans, two Stanford professors. It's smart and, unlike many other such books, it's tactical. But it's been out since 2016, and if you haven't read it yet, you probably won't. It's a very successful book, and I recommend it, but I can't help but wonder if part of its success comes from being targeted most at the people who need it *least*.

This brings me to the final reason you should listen to what I have to say in this book—I wrote it for *you*.

Here's what I know about you:

1. You're already ahead of the game, creating your ideal life because right now—right this second—you're spending your time in a way that's meaningful to you. Meaning derives from purpose. If your purpose in reading this book

---

†   Vistage is a professional development and mentorship program for successful people looking to improve upon and leverage their high levels of performance. Chairs are the leadership guides, or mentors, in this space.

is to figure out your purpose in life, you're serving your purpose by reading. Well done, you.

2. You have questions. Maybe you're in high school or college and thinking about what you want from your professional life and how to get off to the best possible start. Maybe you're a guidance counselor, parent, teacher, or mentor to young people interested in helping them be intentional about how they launch their working lives.

Or you might be somewhere between the middle and end of your career path and you're thinking about taking a new direction. You might even have found the road forked in a way you weren't expecting. Whether you left the workforce to raise a family or you're looking for something more challenging, more meaningful, or just plain different—no matter where you came from, some big questions have turned up in your life, and you turned to books for help answering them. (Another point in your favor!)

These questions probably include: *What do I want to do? What would I enjoy, be good at, or find meaningful? What am I qualified to do? How can I make enough money? How do I know how much is enough? How do I get from here to there?*

3. This is great!

I understand it may not feel great. I know uncertainty can be uncomfortable. You may feel a little lost or directionless, ready for the grand adventure of your life to begin but not sure what direction to set off in to seek your fortune. Good news: You're already underway. You're on the pathfinding path.

THE QUEST FOR YOUR LIFE'S QUEST IS A QUEST.

If you choose to accept this quest in the form of engaging with *Don't Settle*, we'll start by investigating the role purpose plays in creating extraordinary work, the prerequisites established by ancient wisdom and current science for a good life, and the most frequent problems people encounter along the way. With that foundation, I'll outline the best framework I've found for figuring out how to get from here to there: the Ikigai model. Then, we'll explore the model's four domains: what you love, what the world needs, what you can get paid for, and what you're good at. Once you've got a handle on the Ikigai model, I'll introduce a new, five-path framework that I think is even better. We'll look at each of those paths, and you'll pick the one that's right for you at this point in your life. If you engage with the Take Action challenges at the end of each chapter (and actually do them), if you go through the framework and dedicate yourself to following through, I promise you will be more content, productive, and joyful by the time you reach the last page—and for the rest of your life.

The decisions you'll make about your future and the relationship between your passions and your career will feel daunting, but if you make them intentionally, plan your work, and work your plan, you won't end up fighting a man with swords. Unless you want to, that is.

PART ONE

Purpose,
Prerequisites,
and Problems

CHAPTER 1

The Ideal Life

Many people, when they think about their future, ask something like: *What do I want to do with my life?* There are two problems with this question. First, there's an easy answer and it's also a total conversation-killer: "I just want to be happy." Second, the question sounds more confrontational than it needs to. The question I like to ask instead is: *What does your ideal life look like?*

I think this is a great question. It fires up the imagination and helps surface priorities, but it's not necessarily easy to answer. Phrasing the question this way assumes a certain amount of self-knowledge that not everybody has, which often catches people off-guard. I've asked it of folks who range in age from seven to seventy, and not many have had an answer they'd already put time into. But if you don't know where you want to go, how will you get there? Short answer: You won't.

So let's get intentional.

I'm going to make a few key assumptions here about your ideal life:

- You want to be happy.*

- You're mentally healthy enough that the standard prerequisites for happiness apply to you.

- You'll sleep for about a third of your life and will need to spend at least another third of it earning money (or getting an education that will allow you to earn money) to support yourself.

With at least a third of your waking hours earmarked for the work you do to earn a living, it has an outsized impact on your quality of life. If you're going to be intentional about it, and you should be, we're going to need to solve for purpose, because purpose and intention are so closely linked.

---

*   I'm using the word "happy" as a shortcut for a more complex sense of well-being than the word necessarily connotes. Nutella makes me happy, but it's not what makes my life worthwhile. I think when most people say they want to be happy, what they mean is they want to wake up in the morning feeling more anticipation than dread. They want a life that feels like it matters with a very high baseline and spikes of joy on top. I like "happiness" better than "contentment" or "satisfaction" because both those words imply a kind of complacency that I'm not interested in. I'm too excited about what comes next. But when I talk about happiness, understand I don't expect you to be giddy with joy all the time. I mean you can live a life of daily contentment and productivity with more than occasional moments of joy.

Purpose

One of the things I identified early in life and have pursued consistently is having a sense of purpose or meaning. It's certainly possible to live intentionally but not meaningfully, but you can't have a meaningful life without being intentional about it.

Maybe once upon a time, meaning came prepackaged with being born into any of the major religious traditions, but for most people I've met, meaning needs to be constructed deliberately. I've already said that I'm one of the happiest people I know and that several things contributed to that: a wide circle of friends, a close and loving family, the ability to see the upside in almost any situation, a high level of physical fitness, a love of and enjoyment in learning, and the fact that I spend my days doing work I love. All of this is true, but it all also distills into a single thing—I'm living my life purpose.

The core of the way I do everything, personally, is to contribute to an uptick of joy in others. It's why I raise my kids at the juncture of support and challenge, why I mentor entrepreneurs, and why I run a ren faire, a summer camp, and a nonprofit. It's also why I wrote this book. If I can help you align how you make a living with something that you're passionate about, it's going to lead to an increase in joy for you.

As the owner of Sherwood Forest Faire, I get to bring a day of joy to 150,000 people over seventeen days every spring. Here, I'm interested in a much longer timeframe—a joyful life requires more than the usual ren faire fare of turkey legs and mead, even for me. Of course, good food

WORK IS THE RENT WE PAY TO LIVE.

and loving relationships are a huge part of what contributes to my happiness and to my definition of a good life, but smart people for thousands of years have been pondering what else goes on the list.

PASSION IS A PART OF PURPOSE

Everyone from Arnold Schwarzenegger to Cinderella will tell you to follow your passions and believe in your dreams, but there's a growing body of research that suggests that you're better off pursuing something you're good at, or that you can reframe any job as a "calling." But since this is *my* book, here's what I believe you should do about passion, purpose, and profession:

- Have something, or some things, you're passionate about.

- Understand your need for financial security.

- Spend your time in ways that are meaningful to you.

- Align your passion and your work now if your need for financial security is low and you know what your passion is.

- Otherwise, make a plan to build the skills, capital, and network to align your work and passion later on in life.

- If you don't know what your passion is, figure it out. (See Chapter 5, "What Are You Passionate About?")

- If you see no chance ever to align your passion and your work, then be sure to invest in your passion in your free time and keep an open mind to aligning your work and passion in the future.

I first encountered the power of the ideal life question in my Vistage group. There were nine of us—all successful CEOs with big goals—and we'd been given the question ahead of time, so we'd all had a chance to prepare. But before I tell you the two things I learned that afternoon, it's your turn.

Take Action on Your Ideal Life
IMAGINE

Close your eyes and try to imagine yourself ten years from now. Imagine that you're happy and that your life feels meaningful, productive, and rewarding. Imagine waking up on a normal Tuesday morning.

- Are you in a house or an apartment?

- In a city or someplace more remote?

- Do you live alone? If not, who lives with you?

- Do you have a morning routine? If so, what does it include?

- Do you work from home, go into an office, or head outside for work?

- What does your typical workday look like?

- Do you spend more time in meetings with other people or working alone?

- What do you do for lunch?

- For dinner?

- Do you socialize after work? With whom and at what level of friendship or other relationship?

Now, imagine it's the weekend.

- Do you take both Saturday and Sunday off?

- What do you do and with whom?

- Where?

- What are the biggest differences between your ideal workdays and days off?

Finally, imagine the vacation you'd take in your ideal future.

- Is it relaxing or packed with travel and activities?

- Who's with you?

- What makes it so great?

- What about this vacation makes it integral to your vision of an ideal life?

PRIORITIZE

To approach what's ideal from another angle, ask yourself what your life would have to include for you to consider it a success. "If I didn't have X, my life would be less than ideal."

Rank the following in order of their importance to you:

- Accomplishment/Mastery

- Balance

- Beauty

- Creativity/Innovation

- Excitement/Adventure

- Family

- Fun

- Independence

- Learning

- Leisure

- Love/Community

- Making a name for yourself

- Making the world a better place

- Peace/Lack of conflict

- Security

- Social status

- Wealth

Look at the most important thing on your list. Would you give up having the second most important thing to have it? How about the third?

For example, if the preceding alphabetized list was *your* list, would you be willing to sacrifice balance to be extraordinarily accomplished in your chosen field of expertise? Would you give up excitement?

Do this until you've refined your list into "must-haves" and "nice-to-haves."

What would an average week look like that included and maintained your must-have ideals? Really, write this down. Do the work. I promise it will help you.

On the day my Vistage group did this exercise, I ended up being at the far end of the circle, so I got to listen to the other eight people in the group share their visions of their ideal futures. Some were highly detailed; others were focused on a single large change they wanted to make. Here's what I said: "Ten years from now, I want my work life to be exactly the way it has been for the last twelve years, and I want it to stay that way until I die."

This isn't to say I don't have goals that I plan to accomplish or new adventures I want to have. I do. But the shape of my life is ideal as it is.

Now, as promised, here are the two things I learned that day:

1. Imagining your ideal life is a great way to start discovering what matters most to you.

2. Living your ideal life is entirely possible. It's just not inevitable.

I wrote this book to help you increase the odds of living your ideal life. I deeply and passionately believe that taking the actions I've laid out and incorporating the key take-aways into your life will go a long way. But there's one more thing you can do that will dramatically increase their power: Share your work.

Mentors, Role Models, and Partners

Bill Damon, who spent fifty years studying how adolescents learn to lead lives they love, claims that no one can be successful without a role model.[1] Specifically, a role model is someone who sets an example of purposefully accomplishing something on behalf of others. It doesn't have to be someone you know personally. It doesn't even have to be a living person, but you need a model you can look to and believe in.

Ideally, you'll also have a mentor. A mentor may also be a role model, but their primary function is to offer advice, encouragement, and perspective. I regularly go back to my alma mater and talk with young business students. At the end of the session, their professor, who's a friend of mine, will encourage the students to connect with me on LinkedIn. "George is a pretty helpful guy," he'll tell them. "If you think you could use some guidance from him, reach out. He'll talk to you." Remember, as a Vistage chair, I'm basically a paid mentor to CEOs, and yet, handed the opportunity to talk with me for free, fewer than one in a hundred follow up on the offer. I think they're just being a bit too polite.

I think many young people simply don't believe successful businesspeople are as willing to be mentors as many of us are. You don't need someone who's doing what you want to do, just someone who's been intentional about creating a life they love and who's willing to share some of their experience with you. And you need to be willing to learn from that experience.[†]

The research on everything from weight loss to wealth creation and sobriety to longevity makes clear the importance of peer and accountability groups.[‡] If you have a workout buddy, you're more likely to get to the gym. If you have a financial accountability partner, you're less likely to overspend. Having an accountability group for working through this book will be a significant advantage. You shouldn't stop reading now. You can find an accountability partner tomorrow.[2]

Take Action on Your Support Network
FIND A MENTOR

Think about the adults in your orbit—not necessarily just the ones you know, but the ones with just one or two degrees of separation from you—and see if you can identify three that might make good mentors. It doesn't matter if they're working in a field you have no interest in or whether they're obviously passionate about what they do. What we're looking for are people who have been and continue to be intentional about their lives and careers. If you're not sure, ask the adults you know

---

[†]   The ability to learn from the experience of others is my working definition of wisdom.

[‡]   The American Society of Training and Development found that people are 65 percent more likely to reach their goals when they've shared them with someone else. Even better, those odds go up to 95 percent when people share their goals with a group that meets regularly to review them.

how they ended up in the jobs they're in. Look for answers that start with, "I knew I wanted to . . ." or "My plan was . . ."

POTENTIAL MENTORS

- Name: _____

- Name: _____

- Name: _____

You can give them this book and ask them to work it with you or simply tell them what you're up to and ask them if they'd take half an hour a week to review each chapter's action items with you. You only need one of the three to say "yes," but it certainly wouldn't hurt to have more! Not only is it useful to get an outsider's perspective, but mentors can also be a great source of inspiration, wisdom, and encouragement.

- Have you secured a mentor?

    ◦ Circle: Yes   No

- If not, what is your actionable plan to find one?

    ◦ Write it here:

_____

_____

_____

_____

_____

- If so, what's your plan for working with them?

  ○ Write it here:

_____

_____

_____

_____

HAVE ROLE MODELS

Read three biographies. Almost anyone who's done something significant enough to have a book written about them will be an example of a person who intentionally set out to accomplish something. Reading biographies gives you a firsthand look at the challenges and difficulties intentional people face, the satisfactions and fulfillment of a purposeful life, and a model of the mindset you'll need to live a life where you don't settle. As you read, think carefully about what you believe made these people successful, what about them you'd like to emulate, and what you think got in their way. When things get difficult, ask yourself what you think your favorites would have done in your situation.

SET UP ACCOUNTABILITY

Find at least one other person to do the work of this book with you. It could be your best friend, a parent or teacher, or anyone else you know who's ambitious and engaged with shaping their own future. It will increase your chances of doing the work and give you someone to be responsible for helping. I'd rather you read this book and do the exercises alone than not at all, but I'm confident an accountability partner would be mutually beneficial.

THREE PEOPLE TO APPROACH ABOUT FORMING AN ACCOUNTABILITY GROUP:

- Name: _____

- Name: _____

- Name: _____

- When and where will you meet?

  _____

  _____

  _____

What you do to earn a living will comprise at least half of your waking life. If you don't want to settle for whatever career path your circumstances, parents, or culture happened to have put you on, you need to be intentional about choosing your own. To do that, you need to take action. You need at least a rough sketch of what your ideal life looks like and one other person: a role model, mentor, or accountability partner to help you. More than anything else, you need a commitment to being or becoming *intentional*.

KEY TAKEAWAYS

- Everyone wants to be happy. But in order to *be* happy, you must be intentional about establishing the critical preconditions for happiness: a purpose and a vision of your ideal future.

- Know what's most important to you and what your ideal life looks like.

- Establish the support structures that will help you keep accountable for living your purpose and achieving your vision.

CHAPTER 2

A Good Life

The only guys allowed to carry guns in the cabins of airplanes, the highest local lawmen of the Old West, and the top rank in many countries' armies are all named after one guy: William Marshall. Marshall, who died over eight hundred years ago, was the fourth son of a minor noble back when first sons were the only ones who could expect to inherit anything beyond a father's blessing. He went on to become the greatest knight who ever lived. He served five different English kings, including the wildly unpopular King John,* who was such a failure as a monarch that when France invaded, half

---

* King John was the younger brother of King Richard the Lionheart. Richard was the character I played in Sherwood Forest Faire for twelve years. Good times!

of England's barons sided with the enemy on the grounds that the French prince was married to John's niece and would probably do a better job.

King John died in the middle of a civil war and under attack by France, leaving a nine-year-old as his heir. The country divided its loyalty between the dead king's son and the invading French prince. Uncertain who to back, and with the direction of the nation in the balance, the top church officials and nobility turned to William Marshall with the history-deciding question, "Who are we going with, the boy or the prince?"

He answered, "The boy," and the entire country fell in line. Such was the power of the respect he commanded; his two words determined who became king and ended a war.

It wasn't the first time.

Several years earlier, after multiple skirmishes and some bad behavior from King John, King Philip II of France[†] set out to reconquer Normandy from the English kings who had ruled there for decades. There was a huge battle—something of a rarity at the time—with William Marshall and other prominent knights all fighting to hold their portion of the line. It wasn't going well. France was walloping the English, who were losing on almost every side. *Almost* every side. William Marshall and his men were holding their own. And someone noticed and sent up the shout, "This way, men—God is with the marshal!" and it turned the whole tide of the battle.

[†]   This is who my friend Nox played in the theater and why I got to swordfight him.

Why did William Marshall's presence on the battlefield or his verdict on who would be king carry such weight? What made him the greatest knight who ever lived? The same things that make any life great. Marshall had met his standard prerequisites, and so can you.

The Standard Prerequisites

There are a few things most philosophies, religions, and psychologists agree are necessary conditions for happiness: love, health, play, and work. Importantly, the mix of energy balanced across these four elements can ebb and flow with time. For example, you may invest relatively more in work in your twenties and thirties and relatively more in play in your fifties and onward. So long as you are mindful in addressing each of these categories, the amount of effort you put into each can shift to meet your needs over time.

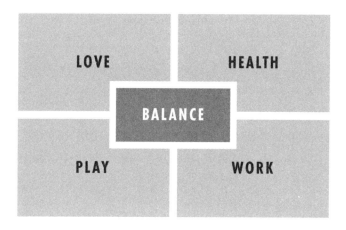

Figure 2.1 Balance Puzzle

LOVE

You don't need to come from a perfect—or even functional—family or have a massive group of friends, but if there aren't a few people in your life who love you and who you love, you aren't going to be happy. Many psychologists will tell you that no decision in life has a greater bearing on your overall happiness than choosing the right spouse. I've known plenty of people with messy families of origin who were happy, but I've never known anyone in a bad marriage with a great life.

My parents got divorced when I was young, and Dad was an alcoholic. But I partnered exceptionally well and have great kids, and in the big picture of my life, that more than makes up for it. This isn't to say a great life necessarily involves romantic love or having children, but it must include loving relationships with people. This isn't just my opinion. The Harvard Study of Adult Development[1]—begun in 1938 and still ongoing—is the longest-running study of happiness to date. It tracked a group of men for over seventy years. One of its most profound conclusions was that more than anything else, happiness is driven by the quantity and quality of relationships with friends and family.

Like good physical health, it can be easy to take good relationships for granted, but a little maintenance can go a long way. As you work on building your ideal life, don't forget to invest and reinvest in love. Absolutely nothing else you accomplish will matter if you don't.

HEALTH

I'm not saying that you can't lead a meaningful or even happy life if you're sick a lot or suffer from chronic illness, but being ill or in pain gets in the way of enjoying life. To be happy, you need to have your basic physical needs met—clean water, enough food, adequate shelter, and a general absence of doubt about whether you'll survive to see the next sunrise. If you already have all this stuff and your body is healthy enough that you're not regularly in pain, take a minute to be happy about it.

If you're young, you might be able to eat like crap, get no exercise, and stay up all night without feeling bad, but it won't last, and you'll be healthier and feel even better if you start taking care of yourself. Because why not? You're the only you that you're going to get.

PLAY

Every Saturday and Sunday morning for fourteen weeks in a row, I show up at 8:15 in the morning for dance rehearsal. Do I always want to be there that early? No. Could I get away with missing it? Yes. Is it work? Hell no! I'm having a ball—literally.

An old quote attributed to everyone from Confucius to Mark Twain advises, "Find a job you enjoy doing, and you will never have to work a day in your life." I never bought into the false dichotomy between work and play. Sometimes the things you do for fun are hard work, and sometimes the things you do for work are so much fun that you'd do them for free. We'll talk a lot more about getting paid to have fun, but it's important to point out the obvious but somehow often-overlooked truth that a life without things you enjoy can't be a happy one.

For our purposes then, I'm going to define "play" as anything you do for its own sake and "work" as anything you do to achieve an outcome. Doing the laundry is work. If it didn't result in clean clothes, I wouldn't do it. I get paid for mentoring CEOs as a Vistage chair, but I'd probably do it for free,[‡] so it isn't work. It's play.

In Chapter 5, "What Are You Passionate About?," I'll make a distinction between pleasure and passion, and there could be one here to draw between pleasure and play, but the big idea is to acknowledge that basic happiness requires moments of feeling good. You need to make sure there are sources of pleasure and fun in your life.

This requires knowing what you actually enjoy. I said earlier that Nutella makes me happy. So does drinking mead. Learning new things makes me happy. So does building a mathematical model that predicts attendance at the faire. So does dancing.

Some pleasures have a limit. One spoonful of Nutella makes me happy, six would not. Other pleasures have an associated pain. Three bottles of mead might make me very happy

----

‡   In theory, I'd do it for free because I find it intrinsically enjoyable and because it fulfills some of my need to be of service to others (more on this in the next section). In practice, however, I wouldn't mentor CEOs for free or even for cheap because they'd place less value on my expertise if they paid less for it.

for a while, but I'd pay for it later in a way I wouldn't enjoy, so I stop drinking before I stop enjoying my drinks.

Pleasure comes in different flavors too. After I've had fun working (playing?) with my faire-attendance model, I'll get more pleasure from dancing than from reading because shifting between physical and mental, solitary and social pleasures increases my enjoyment of them.

I think sometimes, people—particularly young people—have the idea that being an adult means you stop having fun. In fact, the opposite can and should be true. The older you get, the more freedom you'll have to do more of what you enjoy, and the deeper your understanding will be of what's actually fun for you.

WORK

I'm not a big believer in fate or destiny. I don't believe there's just one thing you were born to do or one person you're destined to love. I do believe that people need to feel like their lives have meaning and that they're contributing to something larger than themselves.[§] In other words, while you may not have been born with a pre-ordained purpose, you were born with an innate *need* for one. It sounds like the set-up for a cruel cosmic joke, but it isn't.

---

§   This is the core thesis of Bill Damon's excellent book, *The Path to Purpose*. I highly recommend it, but if you're not inclined to read the whole thing, there's an excellent high-level summary here: https://parentotheca.com/2021/02/24/the-path-to-purpose-william-damon-book-summary.

Of course, you're not doomed to live unfulfilled until you discover your purpose. Purpose isn't something you find; it's something you *create*. In the words of self-help author Mark Manson, "To live a healthy and happy life, we must hold onto values that are greater than our own pleasure or satisfaction. So pick a problem and start saving the world. There's plenty to choose from."[2] That said, building and articulating a purpose for your life isn't necessarily easy or straightforward. Bill Damon captures the internal tension of this work beautifully:

> Young people must discover their own unique purposes out of their own particular interests and beliefs. Yet their discoveries are guided by other people in their lives, and the purposes that they discover are inevitably shaped by values that they encounter in the culture around them. The paradox is that purpose is both a deeply individual and an unavoidably social phenomenon.[3]

Happily, he also says that "*anyone can find purpose and pursue it with rich benefit to themselves and others.*" He even says it in italics!

In a way, there is something funny about purpose because it means that to serve yourself, you have to serve others. To be happy, you need to feel like your life matters. To who? It doesn't matter as long as it's someone other than just you. How? That doesn't matter either. Sure, it can be by donating to charity or curing cancer, but if your art matters to others or the way you wait tables makes a difference in people's lives, that counts, too. A Starbucks barista brings a moment of contentment to hundreds of people a day. That seems like a good use of time.

Take Action on Being of Service to Others
HELP HELPERS

Find something important (or upsetting) to you—an ideal or organization, a particular population or cause. Then find local organizations that are already working in that area.

- **Find your focus.** Try searching the internet for 501(c)3 + [the important ideal or cause] + "near me"

  - For example: 501(c)3 + global warming + "near me"

  - 501(c)3 + PETA + "near me"

  - 501(c)3 + homelessness + "near me"

- **Narrow down your list.** Write down the names of at least two you'd like to contact and start planning what you'll say:

  - Find a way you can contribute (or, in business-speak, "add value").

  - Ask yourself what you have of value. Is it your time, your physical or mental energy, your expertise, skills, or passion?

○ List the kinds of value you might add:

_____

_____

_____

_____

_____

_____

- **Get in touch**. Most of these organizations will have a "get involved" section on their websites, but if they don't, email them anyway. Tell them you want to help and list the value you can add.

HELP PEOPLE

Assuming you care about your family, what can you do to help your parents or siblings? Practice perspective-taking[1]—trying to see things from other people's points of view—but don't be afraid to ask the people you care about what you could do to make their lives a little better.

---

[1] See the "Emotional Intelligence" section in Chapter 7 for a more detailed explanation and a great example of perspective-taking.

LIST THREE WAYS YOU COULD CONTRIBUTE.**

1. _____

2. _____

3. _____

Whether you want to work with an organization or add value in less formal ways (or both!), make a commitment to a weekly practice of doing whatever it is—whether it's calling your grandma and listening to her stories, mowing the neighbor's yard, volunteering at the animal shelter, or helping to get out the vote. Do it long enough that people start to count on you, and see how it feels. If you do both those things—help others *and* reflect on it—you're statistically likely to have "a better attitude to others and do better in school," according to research cited in the wonderfully named *How to Raise Kids Who Aren't Assholes.*[4]

Area of service	
Value you'll add	
Length of contribution	

** Remember to keep these actionable. Not "be nicer to my little sister," but "help Cora with her homework two afternoons a week." Not "help out more around the house," but "take the trash out every Wednesday before being asked."

HELP YOURSELF

If you're finding a sense of purpose elusive, I recommend taking Bill Damon's Youth Purpose Questionnaire, which can be found in the appendix of *The Path to Purpose*.[5]

Agency

There's something psychologists call "learned helplessness," which the folks who named it studied by delivering electric shocks to dogs. (I know, *the bastards!*) The experiment went like this: Put a dog in a cage, electrify half the floor, then watch the dog walk over to the other half of the cage. This is a dog with *agency*. It can solve the problem of the ouchy floor. Eventually, if a red light signals that the floor is about to be electrified, the dog will walk over to the unlit half and avoid getting shocked altogether. Even better.

Now, electrify the whole floor or randomize the association between the light and the shock, and pretty soon, the dog will just lie there and suffer. Cause and effect have broken down. Puppy learned that nothing it does will solve the problem of the electrified floor. It's learned it is helpless. This dog cannot be happy.

Humans are just the same. To be happy, we need to believe in our ability to cause effects. We need to have agency.

I put a lot of energy into the marketing of Sherwood Forest Faire. Every year, we buy dozens of billboards and print ads, thousands of radio and TV spots, and even more digital ads on Facebook, Instagram, TikTok, YouTube, and Google. And I track it all against ticket sales. I know the ROI (return on investment) for each ad. In other words, I can see the effect each ad causes. It may be a little nerdy, but I find it extremely satisfying.

Agency itself is value-neutral. It just means the ability to make something happen—to produce an outcome. Whether or not you like the outcome you produce is a different matter. A mental health counselor friend of mine says that he spends more time convincing his clients they have agency than anything else. What I've found to be true in my life is that people usually have more agency than they think. It's the opposite of what Paulo Coelho[6] identifies as "the world's greatest lie" in *The Alchemist*.[††] So how about trusting us for a bit and assuming that you can effect major positive changes in your life? You'll be glad you did.

If you need more evidence to give up your oh-so-fashionable nihilism for a bit and believe that you—yes, you—can make a real difference, I submit the story of Ruth Bader Ginsberg (RBG).[‡‡] Despite being the first person, male or female, to become a member of both the Harvard and the Columbia law reviews while she was in law school and graduating first in her class, no law firm would hire her.[7] She worked first as a clerk for a judge and then as a research assistant, and went to war on the sexism baked into the language of the law.

Ginsberg identified thousands of state and federal statutes

[††] According to Coelho, the world's greatest lie is "that at a certain point in our lives, we lose control of what's happening to us, and our lives become controlled by fate."

[‡‡] I highly recommend the 2018 documentary *RBG*.

that discriminated on the basis of sex and filed lawsuits to get them struck down.[§§] She was determined to make a difference. And she did, one bad law at a time. Intentionally. By the time Ginsberg was nominated for the Supreme Court, she'd earned such widespread respect that she was confirmed by a vote of ninety-six to three. RBG . . . a modern-day William Marshall.

If there's only one thing I can convince you of, let it be this: *Be intentional.* Don't default into your own life. Make deliberate choices and act on them. Yes, it can be scary and yes, it takes more work than just going with the flow, but it's the shortest route to a joyful, productive, and contented life. And it's the only way to really own your own life.

DON'T WORK ON BEING HAPPY. WORK ON BEING INTENTIONAL.

Being intentional about your career path means not letting the economy, your parents, or your peers make decisions for you. If you've made deliberate choices and acted on them, you're less likely to second-guess yourself later or to waste time and energy wondering whether you're in the right line of work. This isn't to say you may not later change your mind or that you might not be wrong now about what you'll want later, but by making intentional choices, you won't have the constant low-level anxiety of wondering about the path you're on. You'll know because you explicitly chose it.

[§§] A few real gems: The husband decides where the family lives and the wife is obligated to follow him. In twelve states, husbands could not be prosecuted for raping their wives. Women could not get credit cards in their own names.

KEY TAKEAWAYS

- A good life requires balancing health, love, play, and purposeful work, but the balance among these four may shift over time.

- Purpose isn't something the right job brings to your life, it's something you bring to your work.

- Helping others helps you. Being of service and meeting other people's needs is often enough to create a sense of purpose.

- Helping yourself (acting with agency) helps, too. Exercise the control you have where you have it, and you'll find those areas get bigger.

CHAPTER 3

Being Intentional

You make hundreds of choices every day. Some are deliberate: You decide to order a pizza and choose the toppings you want. Many other choices are out-sourced to habits: You don't make the decision to brush your teeth when you get out of bed, you just do it—or at least I hope you do! But some of the choices you make aren't really *chosen*. If you've ever found yourself halfway through a bag of chips you hadn't intended to eat or hours down a meme hole when you actually meant to be studying, you know what I mean. I'm not here to shame you. It happens to the best of us. But each time it does, we give up some of our power.

I want you to be powerful. I want you to take as much control over your life as you can wrest from it. I want you to make choices, even when you're uncertain, even if they may turn out to be wrong, because making choices makes you powerful.* I want you to appoint yourself the creator of your world, your life, and your future. And for that, you need EPO.

EPO is an initialism I made up as a memory aid for Expectation, Persistence, and Ownership. (I almost used the word "grit" instead of "persistence" and called my mnemonic "EGO," as in Latin for "I." But seeing as I've long said the male ego is responsible for at least 80 percent of what's wrong with the world, I couldn't bring myself to use the word in a positive light.) Even though the initialism is made up, each letter stands for an idea that many great historical figures, scientists, philosophers, and psychologists endorse.

Expectation

In the famous words of Henry Ford: "Whether you think you can or think you can't, you're right." I'm not going to pump you up on the power of positive thinking or tell you that you can manifest whatever by talking to yourself in the mirror, but I do think there's a strong case to be made for deliberate optimism.

Belief is a choice. What you believe about yourself, your possibilities, and your future is just one more decision you can make intentionally or default into. If you're in the habit of thinking negative thoughts, it's not because they're true. It's because you've developed that habit.

---

* I like the way Matthew McConaughey makes this point in his memoir, *Greenlights*: "Sometimes which choice you make is not as important as making a choice and committing to it."

Either way, there are some compelling reasons to stop. First of all, thinking positive thoughts just feels better than thinking negative ones. How you think about things changes your experience. And you don't have to take my word for it:

"The mind is its own place and in itself can make a heaven of hell, a hell of heaven."

—John Milton

"There's nothing good or bad but thinking makes it so."

—William Shakespeare

"Your worst enemy cannot harm you as much as your own thoughts unguarded, but once mastered, no one can help you as much, not even your father or your mother."

—Buddha

Or, if you want to be more modern and scientific, Aaron Beck, one of the "five most influential psychotherapists of all time"[1] described a negative feedback loop in which negative thoughts cause negative feelings, which then color perceptions of the world, causing negative thoughts, which cause negative feelings. And around and around we go, spiraling all the way down into Hell.

However, if we practice looking on the bright side: "It is possible to break the disempowering feedback cycle between negative beliefs and negative emotions. If you can get people to examine those beliefs and consider counterevidence, it gives them at least some moment of relief from negative emotions.

And if you release them from negative emotions, they become more open to questioning their negative beliefs."[2]

In his powerful and influential book *Positive Intelligence*, author and coach Shirzad Chamine says he encourages his clients to look at everything bad that happens as a gift. He asks them to write down three possible good results of any negative event. He gets a lot of pushback. People insist that nothing good can result from their problems, but almost inevitably, if they do the exercise, they're able to find at least one outcome that some action on their part could cause.

As for myself, I either picked up the optimism habit early or it was simply my default outlook. For example, I met a friend for a work session the other day and I wasn't feeling well. The bright side I found? We're often more creative when we're tired, so maybe I'd have more new ideas feeling sluggish! And I did.

You've probably heard the expression "rose-colored glasses," which implies a kind of blind optimism, one that isn't very useful. You don't want to ignore problems—they're valuable sources of information. I recommend building yourself some "silver-lining glasses" instead. When things don't go your way or you run into difficulties, practice being intentional by making the deliberate choice to look for an upside.

Another takeaway from Shirzad Chamine's Positive Intelligence movement is that negative thoughts are useful *for one second*. Beyond that, they aren't useful anymore, they're just painful. So, recognize your negative thoughts, name them, separate yourself from the thought, and set the thought aside. In Shirzad's teaching, focusing relentlessly for a couple of minutes on physical sensations helps you to externalize the negative emotion. By externalize, I mean this: The negative emotion isn't *you*. You are the awareness of the emotion. You can set the emotion aside. This takes work. If you do the work, you build muscle memory and it becomes second nature.

Take Action on Practicing Great Expectations

1. For the next twenty-four hours, pay attention to any time you feel disappointed or pissed off. Each time, look for a silver lining.

2. Think of the last time something didn't go your way. Write it down in the space provided, then write three possible positive outcomes.

A quick note before you do: Your first instinct is going to be to argue with me. You're going to think, "There can't possibly be three positives of this really bad thing," but I'm telling you there can be. I'll give you an example from my own life.

In college, I decided that the best career path for me was to land a consulting job with McKinsey and Company as soon as I graduated. Knowing they only hired a few people each year, I spent some time figuring out what they looked for and discovered that the list included your SAT scores. In high school, I hadn't taken the SAT seriously because I knew admission to the college I wanted to attend was based on class rank, and I'd been told I was ranked second in my class.

I was excited to be the salutatorian but when the final rankings came out at the end of the spring semester, I was third. All my grades were in the high nineties. How could

I have missed the number two spot? There's valedictorian, salutatorian, and everybody else. I was devastated. I drove home and sat alone in my Oldsmobile and cried. I know, poor George, but I was really heartbroken and confused. As it turns out, the woman who'd unseated me had taken an honors class which, unbeknownst to me, added ten points to her grade in that class.

If you'd asked me at the time, I probably would have insisted that there was absolutely no silver lining to the situation. But there was. I learned a powerful lesson from that disappointment: *If you want something, know the rules for getting it.* That's why, in college, when I wanted a job at McKinsey, I learned what their hiring rules were and knew in plenty of time that I'd need to study, retake the SAT, and crush it. I did, graduated (top of my class, thank you very much), turned in my grades and my board scores, and got the job.

Now, with that in mind, write your example and three possible positive outcomes in the following space:

Persistence

Persistence is what you need when optimism runs headlong into reality. Finding the silver lining is a great first step, but to keep on stepping, it's important to cultivate a way of talking to yourself about challenges. There are two terrific books on this subject, *Grit* by Angela Duckworth and *Mindset* by Carol Dweck, that I'd summarize very broadly this way: When things go wrong, don't take it personally. Be deliberate about how you frame disappointment or failure. If you're in the habit of thinking things like, "I guess I'm just not cut out for that," or "I'm not good at this," you'll give up. And if those things were true, you'd be right to quit. No point in keeping after something impossible. But way too often, people think not being good at something means they'll *never* be good at it. In fact, almost everybody is bad at everything the first time.

It's much easier to persist in the face of difficulties when you frame setbacks, failures, and negative experiences as excellent markers of things you haven't learned yet. In fact, you can make a meta-skill out of this and get better at getting better at things.

In my first year out of school, I was a mess. I'd landed the job I'd set out to get and I quickly realized I had no idea what I was doing. I was so stressed that my face broke out with acne. My project manager had basically said, "I want you to build a simulation model for the global supply chain of laptop computers. Here's a software package [that you've never heard of]. Figure it out."

I had no idea what to do. Build a model of a global supply chain? I didn't know what that meant! I asked for more direction, but the guy couldn't give it to me. I could easily have decided I just wasn't McKinsey material or that I'd been wrong about strategy consulting. Instead, I was relentless about finding the mentors and resources I needed to accomplish the task. I started asking other people at the firm—people who were clearly productive or a level or two ahead of me—"When did the light bulb come on for you?"

When you're spinning your wheels, ask for help. If the help doesn't help, ask for other people's stories. Operate from the assumption that, no matter what it is, if other people are doing it, you can learn how to do it, too.

If having a growth mindset means you believe you can figure out how to win when you lose, grit means believing losing won't kill you. Maybe you've felt yourself shying away from being intentional as I've described because you're afraid to set goals for yourself and take action on them. Maybe you're worried you won't reach what you aim for and the disappointment of that experience will break you. It won't. In fact, I think you're much more likely to be broken down by the slow deterioration of *not* striving than by taking a shot and missing. Failure and other painful experiences do much less lasting damage than slow rot. Sure, you're less likely to break your leg on the sofa than out running, but you're more likely to die of a heart attack if you don't get out there and try.[†]

You aren't fragile. Like your immune system, you need

[†]   Over time, you're even less likely to break your leg. When astronauts come back from space, their bones are weaker because they've experienced less stress. Too much stress is toxic but too little isn't good for you either.

challenges and exposure to certain kinds of stress to get stronger. Or, to quote my mom, "If you're never failing, you're not setting your sights high enough." Like muscles, we grow when we're pushed. Of course, you can overdo it at the gym and actually hurt yourself. But being intentional requires you to believe that problems are solvable, to see the positives in negative experiences, and to be relentless about getting out there and trying again.

This is going to be controversial, but I think that as a society, we're in danger of overcorrecting a bit on mental health. I have a good friend my age who still struggles with the damaging shame heaped on him for having ADHD. So obviously, that kind of nonsense needed to stop. But as we've stopped shaming people for having brains that work differently and normalized going to therapy, we should be clearheaded about what going too far in the opposite direction looks like. Having ADHD, anxiety, depression, or dyslexia means you have to work harder at certain things than neurotypical people. You deserve compassion and a supportive environment, but not a free pass.[‡] A specific example of overcorrecting would be people using self-diagnosed conditions to make excuses for not doing what they have agreed to do.

---

‡ I'm assuming that my readers are basically mentally healthy, but I want to make it very clear that I'm not saying that some people don't have serious mental health challenges that make their lives very difficult or that anyone should be ashamed about them. If you struggle with severe anxiety or depression, please get qualified professional help. If you need it, the National Suicide and Crisis hotline is always available at 988lifeline.org or by calling 988. Even at its most difficult, your life is worth fighting for.

I have a friend who landed his dream job and got in trouble for showing up high every day. He explained to his boss that he had anxiety and was treating it with weed. He genuinely believed his employer needed to respect his mental health issues and be okay with him smoking at work. She wasn't. My friend kept showing up high and got fired. After getting fired from another job or two for the same thing, reality finally smacked him across the face. He's now completely sober, productive, and far more content than he's ever been. He has also confessed to himself, and to me, that his self-diagnosed anxiety was BS. He just liked being high.

I'm not trying to say that anxiety disorders aren't real. They clearly are. But he had diagnosed himself, and I'm not sure he wasn't just pathologizing some of the normal worries of life. Nobody's happy all the time. Not even me. But feeling sad or down or unhappy doesn't mean you have clinical depression any more than feeling nervous or awkward means you have anxiety. Don't diagnose yourself. You can have a hypothesis, of course, but get a pro to confirm it.

A similar phenomenon crops up in parenting, where the research is really clear that children need both high standards and support, but the trend has been to move away from asking too much of kids. If your parents were great at making you feel loved, but not so big on asking a lot of you, then you may have experienced some difficulty in your adult life when it comes to goal-setting, consistency, and success.

Laurence Steinberg, one of the world's leading experts on adolescence, has zeroed in on the relationship between parenting style and success. Angela Duckworth, in her seminal book *Grit*, captures her interpretation of it in a 2x2 grid:

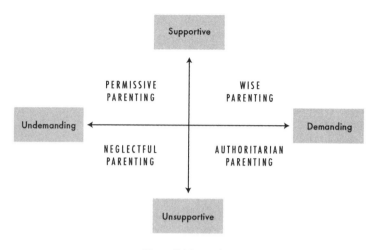

Figure 3.1 Parenting

This bit of wisdom has the highest should-be-known to actually known ratio of any intellectual insight I'm aware of.

Take Action by Building Persistence

1. Take Angela Duckworth's Grit questionnaire here: https://angeladuckworth.com/grit-scale. If you're not happy with your score, it's time to flex your growth mindset. Duckworth says there are two ways to grow your grit:

    a. **From the inside out** by cultivating your interests (see Chapter 5 of this book, "What Are You Passionate About?"), developing a habit of "challenge-exceeding-skill" practice (see the following seven Take Action items), by connecting your work to a purpose beyond yourself (see Chapter 2, "A Good Life"), and by learning to hope when all seems lost (see Chapter 3, "Being Intentional").

b. **From the outside in** by seeking external challenge and support from family, mentors, and accountability groups (see Chapter 1, "The Ideal Life").[3]

2. Have you had enough experience with losing or failing to know it won't kill you? If you haven't, consider raising the bar for yourself. What's a level of accomplishment that you think you can't hit? Straight As? Getting in to an Ivy League school? Making the varsity team?

Stretch goal: _____

_____

_____

_____

Try for it. Don't try to fail but try knowing that you *may* fail and that if you do, you've gotten some valuable experience.

3. Have you ever given up too soon? When?

Take a few minutes to describe why you quit, why you think you could have persisted longer, and what might have been different if you had.

_____

_____

_____

_____

4. When in your life have you persisted? Write an account of a time when you didn't quit. Why were you tempted to give up? How did you manage to keep going? Hold on to this memory and take the time to identify with it. You are persistent. You have proven this to yourself.

_____

_____

_____

_____

_____

_____

5. What accomplishment in your life are you proudest of? Describe it. How hard did you work to achieve it? What gave you the persistence to keep going when it got difficult?

_____

_____

_____

_____

_____

_____

6. If you had trouble answering the two previous questions because you can't see times in your life when you've persisted or made yourself proud, commit right now to finishing this book. It won't be easy, but if you do, I promise you can feel proud of that accomplishment.

7. If you want a shorter-term win, for the next week, commit to watching one TED Talk every day before you watch anything else on YouTube or TikTok, or before playing a video game, play ten minutes with a ball—basket, soccer, juggling, ping-pong, or any kind of ball at all!

8. If you've been diagnosed with anxiety or depression by a medical professional (and even if you haven't!) conduct any or all of the following week-long experiments on yourself. This is a great opportunity to work with your accountability partner.

- Cut out social media for a week.

- Cut out sugar for a week.

- Take a half-hour walk outside every day for a week.

- Get eight hours of sleep every night for a week.

- Drink no alcohol for a week.

- Smoke no weed for a week.

At the beginning of each week's experiment, rate your overall level of happiness on a scale from one to ten or take an online mood assessment.[§] Do each of these for a week and at the end of six weeks, you might just feel amazing.

As part of the experiment, log your activity (or lack thereof) in the table below:

	Starting Score	M	T	W	Th	F	St	Sn	Final Score
No social media									
Sugar-free									
½ hour walk									
Sleep 8 hours									
Alcohol-free									
Weed-free									

As you're logging your activity, notice when you find it particularly easy or difficult to stick to your plan. What helps when it gets hard? What makes it more difficult? Would a role model, mentor, or accountability partner help?

Do any of these suggested experiments seem undoable to you? If they do, think about why and consider talking to someone you trust about how you might make them more achievable. Remember, there's a direct link between doing something difficult and feeling good about yourself.

---

§ This one from the UK's National Health Service is a good one: https://talk2gether.nhs.uk/quick-self-assessment/.

Ownership

Ownership, at its most fundamental, is a mindset. In Carol Dweck's *The Growth Mindset,* she outlines two ways of thinking: the "growth mindset" and the "fixed mindset." These two paradigms stand in opposition to one another, and only one of them will lead to personal growth and success. (I'll let you guess which one.) In the same way, ownership, as a mindset, stands in opposition to the victim mentality. Some models use "creators" as shorthand for people who claim ownership over their own lives, and the distinction between them and "victims" is pretty stark.

VICTIMS SAY:	CREATORS SAY:
"It's not my fault."	"I take responsibility."
"I have to."	"I choose to."
"You made me mad."	"I lost my temper."
"I can't."	"I won't."
"There's nothing I can do."	"I can always choose my response."

As you can see in the preceding responses, from the victim mindset, things happen *to* you. You're at the mercy of your upbringing, under other people's control, and powerless in the face of adverse circumstances.[¶] Please understand the difference between being a victim and being *victimized*. Reminding a person that they have ownership over what happens to them is *not* the same as saying it's their fault if someone assaults

---

¶ There's an excellent summary of these two mindsets here: https://www. visionstoexcellence.com/powerful-mindsets-owner-vs-victim/.

them. Nobody is ever "asking for it." But everyone—even a person who has been the victim of someone else's brutality, adverse childhood events (ACEs), racism, or systemic violence—has a choice to make. The Austrian psychiatrist and Holocaust survivor Viktor Frankl, during his time in a Nazi concentration camp, came to think of this choice as "the last human freedom."[4]

When I talk about ownership, I am combining two ideas from the world of psychology: "locus of control" and "bias toward action." Without getting overly technical, my definition of "ownership" is putting yourself in the driver's seat of your life. Or, in the immortal (if slightly modified) words of William Ernest Henley: Knowing that you are the master of your fate, you are the captain of your soul.**

Most people don't do this. Be exceptional.

How isn't obvious or easy, but it is natural. Human beings, I believe, were born to be the creators of their own lives, but there are a few things about how our minds evolved and the way our society functions that can get in the way. I call them "shitty thinking habits." Learning to recognize and deal with them will not only help you get the most out of this book, it'll make your whole life better and you, happier.

** This is a line from *Invictus*, Henley's anthem to agency, which Nelson Mandala famously repeated to himself during his years in prison.

Take Action on Increasing Ownership

In a minute, I'm going to go through a list of shitty thinking habits that I've synthesized from a variety of sources. To make what you'll learn more actionable and personal, take a minute to fill in your answers to the following questions:

1. How many extracurricular activities do you do? Include everything you might put on a college application or resume: sports, clubs, service organizations, jobs, etc.

    Number of Extracurriculars: _____

    How many of them did you choose yourself because you wanted to do them? _____

    How many were chosen for you? _____

2. On a one-to-ten scale, how much ownership do you feel over your life and your future?

    1 = No ownership, other people or circumstances control my present and future.

    10 = Total ownership, I, and I alone, control my present and my future.

    1   2   3   4   5   6   7   8   9   10

3. Put a reminder in the calendar on your phone to come back and score this again in a month.

    1   2   3   4   5   6   7   8   9   10

4. If your answer is less than eight, list at least three specific things that are getting in your way and your next step to overcome those three barriers.

   1. _____

   2. _____

   3. _____

5. What are you proudest of? What goals have you set and reached? Write down your top three life accomplishments so far. (And yes, you must think of three.)

   1. _____

   2. _____

   3. _____

6. Were any of the barriers you listed in #4 in place when you accomplished the items in #5? If so, what enabled you to overcome them then? Are there people who have had similar impediments but done what you intend anyway?

   _____

   _____

   _____

   _____

   _____

7. Do you ever find yourself thinking thoughts that start with, "I'll never," "I'll always," "I can't," or "I have"? Write down the rest of the thought(s):

_____

_____

_____

_____

_____

Ask yourself: How might this thought be wrong? Just becoming aware of how frequently (or infrequently!) hallmark victim language comes out of your mouth (or in your self-talk) can be an incredibly useful exercise.

8. Start taking ownership of your future right now. If you didn't do the Intentionality table in the introduction, do it now.

KEY TAKEAWAY

- Being intentional requires actively practicing optimism, building persistence, and increasing ownership.

CHAPTER 4

Avoiding Pitfalls

You are the creator of your life. You can deliberately work toward making one that's as close to your ideal as possible, or you can forfeit your power and allow your creation to be shaped by forces that feel—but aren't—out of your control. Life may throw you curveballs, but if you expect great things and learn to mine the inevitable setbacks and adversities for their silver linings, you can keep going through "whatever hell may be"* and not set up camp there. Then, with optimism and grit, you can take on the shitty thinking habits that get in your way and intentionally choose a career path that accounts for both passion and financial security.

---

* Another nod to Henley's *Invictus*.

Cognitive Distortions

In *The Coddling of the American Mind*, authors Greg Lukianoff and Jonathan Haidt make the claim that just reading the book *Feeling Good* by David Burns has been clinically shown to be an effective treatment for depression. In *Feeling Good*, Burns outlines a host of what he calls "cognitive distortions," which is really just a way of saying twisted thinking.[1] I've cherry-picked the cognitive distortions I think are most likely to keep people from taking ownership of their lives and being intentional about their futures.

EMOTIONAL REASONING

This means believing what you feel. If, as an example, you feel bored, you think that means the thing you're doing is boring. Or, you might believe that not feeling like brushing your teeth is a good reason not to pick up your toothbrush. For our purposes in this book, it'd be like saying, "I don't feel like I'm the creator of my own life, so I must not be."

CATASTROPHIZING

This is what happens when you wear your silver lining glasses backwards. If you absolutely know in your heart that if you don't get into your first-choice college you're going to end up living under a bridge, or if you keep replaying that one awkward comment you made to someone and spinning a future of social rejection and isolation, then your thinking is distorted by catastrophizing. When people talk about a fear of failure, it's frequently not the failure itself they're afraid of, it's all the catastrophes they expect that failure to set in motion.

OVERGENERALIZING

Everyone overgeneralizes. (See what I did there?) It means taking one or even several outcomes and assuming they're the inevitable result of any input: "I asked three people out, and they all turned me down. I shall be single until death." Or "I tried ice skating once, and I'm bad at it." Or "People from my background/socioeconomic class/family structure/neighborhood aren't successful."

I'm not saying there aren't trends and that certain people may find it more difficult to get a great education and a good job or stay vertical on ice or find dates. I'm saying it's a distortion to believe that it's impossible or inevitable.

BINARY THINKING

Also known as "black-and-white thinking" or "dichotomous thinking," this distortion tricks you into believing that your life will be a success or a failure, that anyone (including you) is a good person or a bad one, or that any activity or endeavor is worthwhile or worthless. Thinking this way is easier than dealing with all the complicated nuances of a life that's mostly great with the occasional setback or with a person who's great to be around but can't be trusted. But reality simply isn't that simple, and any black-and-white picture of it will be an incomplete one.

LABELING

Labeling is a bit of a combination of binary thinking and overgeneralizing. When you label a job a "good job" or a person a "loser," you're distorting reality and closing down possibilities. The problem with labels is that they're stealth predictions. A loser can never win. A bad day at a good job turns it into a bad job.

Labels don't have to have attached value judgments to be limiting. Nobody wants to be a loser, but if you accept the label "jock" or "queen bee" or even "good student," you're boxing yourself in. Without getting into identity politics, the same is true for other kinds of labels. Labels can also be implied. The thought, *I'm not the kind of person who . . .* is an excellent indication of a maybe unarticulated label you've assigned yourself. Be who you are. All of who you are. Your name is all the label you need.

BLAME

If controlling parents are the reason you're not the creator of your life, if racism is why you'll never have the career you want, or if depression is the thing keeping you from being intentional about your future, blame is twisting your thinking. I'm not saying that other people, social systems, and mental health conditions don't affect you. They do. I'm saying that taking ownership of your life means deciding that their impact isn't determinant. This gets back to agency—*you have it!*

TAKE ACTION ON YOUR COGNITIVE DISTORTIONS

Go back to the "Take Action on Increasing Ownership" section and review your answers to #4. Can you spot any of the cognitive distortions we've just discussed on your list?

Which two of the preceding cognitive distortions are most familiar to you? Make a plan to start addressing them today. Extra points if that plan includes enlisting a mentor or accountability partner to watch out for them in you and giving them explicit permission to call you out on them when they see it in you.

Internal Saboteurs

In *Positive Intelligence*, Shirzad Chamine identifies ten shitty thinking habits personified as judge, victim, pleaser, restless, hyper-vigilant, hyper-achiever, hyper-rational, controller, stickler, and avoider. He contrasts them with the sage—the highest and best part of yourself. There's a free assessment at Chamine's website (www.positiveintelligence.com) that you can take to help identify your most prevalent saboteurs, and I recommend his book for the specific exercises he's developed to target each of them. All the saboteurs can mess with the quality of your life, but the following eight are particularly relevant in taking ownership of it.

THE JUDGE

Everyone has this saboteur. It's the voice in your head that points out every mistake or weirdness in you, your friends, your parents, and that guy walking down the street in bad pants. In reality, the Judge isn't really you at all—it's your internalization of society's rules. If your head is full of judgments about how things should be, what people should do, and the life you should have, you're in danger of letting the Judge run your life.

THE VICTIM

We took a pretty detailed look at the victim mentality back in Chapter 3, "Being Intentional," when we talked about ownership. The same definition works well here, too. But as a saboteur, the Victim also becomes almost a composite of all the mental distortions we just talked about. It's that part of you that wants someone else to tell you what to do. It's the part of you that feels helpless and overwhelmed. It's the saboteur that blames other people, past traumas, and social conditions for the way things are. It insists these forces make it impossible for you to be intentional.

THE STICKLER

Similar to the Judge, the Stickler has lots of ideas about the right way to do things. The stickler is perfectionism personified. If you got bogged down on any of the writing exercises because you were trying to get them "just right," or if you've never found a passion because there was always some element of it you didn't like or because you weren't 100 percent sure it was the one for you, this is the saboteur you need to beat.

HYPER-RATIONAL

Being in charge of your life doesn't mean being the emotionally shut-down drill sergeant of it. Learning to manage the emotional reasoning cognitive distortion teaches us not to let our emotions captain the ship of our lives. Confronting the hyper-rational saboteur reminds us that our feelings shouldn't be gagged and bound and thrown into the brig. Emotions and intuition are useful sources of information. Don't miss out on their insights just because they aren't always rational.

CONTROLLER

For the most part, I'm advocating for taking control of your life and your future, but the controller saboteur is on this list for two reasons. First, if your responses to the questions at the start of this section were some version of "I don't need any help from anyone" or "You can't tell me what to do. You're not my dad!" then you may have control issues that will get in your way.

Second, while being intentional will always serve you well, sometimes life doesn't act in accordance with our plans. If you get to college on a soccer scholarship with your whole career planned out and tear your ACL in the first preseason game, you're likely not going to handle it well if you have the controller saboteur. You'll either stick to your plan long past the point that it's feasible and injure yourself further, or you'll throw the whole idea of planning out. The behaviors of learned helplessness that we talked about in the section on agency are often the "might as well"[†] response to disappointment.

If you've had a couple of experiences where your plans didn't work out, it's easy to conclude that there's no point in planning. But as the great philosopher Mike Tyson once said, "Everyone has a plan until they get punched in the mouth." Being intentional doesn't mean being inflexible. You can be intentional about how you handle getting punched in the mouth. I'm pretty sure that's why we've heard of Mike Tyson.

RESTLESS

If you're already bored with this book, welcome to your saboteur. This one's a sneaky devil, and it's most likely to show up when you're getting close to something you've been working toward. The Restless saboteur is why so many entrepreneurs give up on their business just before they start to turn a profit. If they'd only stuck it out for another few months! It's also why people quit diets and exercise programs.

PLEASER

If your plan is to go to med school because Mommy wants you to be a doctor, then your Pleaser saboteur is keeping you from

---

[†] You may recognize this nifty little brain-boil as the linking phrase between thoughts like "I've already blown my diet/budget/sobriety/good habit streak" and "eat the rest of the box of cookies/buy the matching shoes/finish the bottle/stay up all night." Don't fall for it! When you get a paper cut, you don't cut your other hand because you're already bleeding.

taking ownership of your life. If you're trying to make other people happy—or impressed or envious or proud—you're giving their opinion of you power over you. Taking ownership of your life doesn't mean not caring what anyone else thinks, but it does mean recognizing that if you let your mother pick your career path, you're the one responsible if you later realize you hate sick people.

AVOIDER

The Avoider saboteur would like you to consider watching YouTube. This one reminds you that hard things are *hard*. If you know what you should do but don't do it regularly, distract yourself from thinking about your future because it's scary, or if you've stayed in a bad relationship rather than have a tough break-up talk, this saboteur needs your attention. (Although it would also like to remind you that self-improvement is hard and, hey—YouTube!)

SAGE

Chamine uses the designation "Sage Brain" to refer to the best and most fully human aspects of our intelligence. The sage thinks creatively and optimistically and is the source of our empathy, gratitude, curiosity, and equilibrium. It's the you that you want to be. Interestingly, he says about twenty percent of living from this part of yourself, rather than ceding control to your saboteurs, is simply knowing that the sage and saboteur brains *exist*. So, you're welcome.

Chamine offers a six-week course complete with assigned exercises, a custom app, and designated accountability groups, because the other 80 percent is all about practice. The exercises build emotional muscle memory and train you to disarm your saboteurs and strengthen your sage. It's a great course, but it's not free, and you can get everything (except the app and the accountability group) by reading his book and doing the work on your own.

TAKE ACTION TO DEFEAT YOUR INTERNAL SABOTEURS

1. Go back to the "Take Action on Increasing Ownership" section and look at #4 again. Can you spot any of these saboteurs on your list?

2. Chamine says everyone has the Judge saboteur, but looking back over the list (or having taken the free assessment at www.positiveintelligence.com), which other two have the largest negative impact on your life?

The Judge

_____

_____

How do each of your top three saboteurs show up in your life?

_____

_____

_____

_____

_____

_____

_____

_____

_____

_____

Over the next week, be particularly alert for these patterns of thought and when you notice them, make a point of naming them and then setting them aside. Just the practice of noticing and naming your saboteurs can go a long way toward defeating them.

Intentionality and Ikigai

Shitty thinking habits (cognitive distortions and internal saboteurs) can trick you into thinking you're not the creator of your own life. But once you've made the choice to be intentional, the question is: What do you intend for your life?

As I mentioned previously, my frustration with the lack of *actionable* resources to help young people answer this question is what led to my decision to write this book. Of the many frameworks and toolkits I've explored, I find the Japanese concept of Ikigai is the most useful.

The Ikigai framework consists of four overlapping circles that converge in the center. The four circles are: what you love, what the world needs, what you can get paid for, and what you're good at. The intersection of the first two is Mission, the overlap of the second and third is Vocation, that of the third and fourth is Profession, and the fourth and first is Passion. In the center, where all four converge, is your *Ikigai*—your "reason for being." What a beautiful idea!

IKIGAI

A Japanese concept meaning "a reason for being"

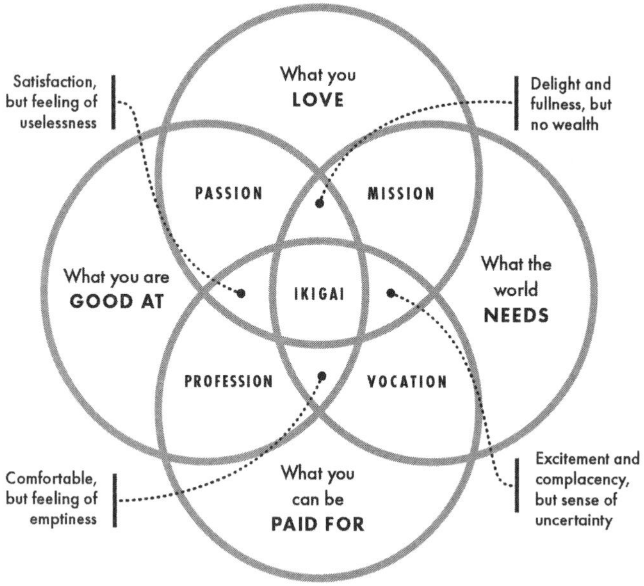

Satisfaction, but feeling of uselessness

What you LOVE

Delight and fullness, but no wealth

PASSION

MISSION

What you are GOOD AT

IKIGAI

What the world NEEDS

PROFESSION

VOCATION

Comfortable, but feeling of emptiness

What you can be PAID FOR

Excitement and complacency, but sense of uncertainty

Figure 4.1 Ikigai

We will explore each circle of the Ikigai framework in the next four chapters. Then I'll introduce a new framework, which I think is even better.

KEY TAKEAWAYS

- Cognitive distortions are patterns of thinking that make it more difficult to take ownership of your life and act intentionally about your future. Spotting your twisted thinking and straightening it out increases your power and happiness and makes it easier to move deliberately toward your ideal life.

- Everyone falls prey to internal mental saboteurs. Learn to recognize the ones you're most susceptible to and get into the practice of refuting them. You'll be happier and more empowered if you do.

- The Ikigai framework says that your reason for being exists at the intersection of what the world needs, what you can get paid for, what you're good at, and what you're passionate about.

PART TWO

Four Circles and a Matrix

CHAPTER 5

What Are You Passionate About?

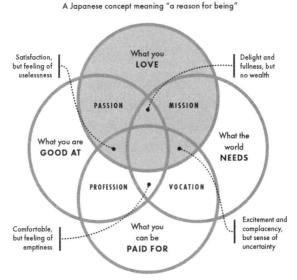

IKIGAI

A Japanese concept meaning "a reason for being"

Satisfaction, but feeling of uselessness

What you **LOVE**

Delight and fullness, but no wealth

PASSION

MISSION

What you are **GOOD AT**

What the world **NEEDS**

PROFESSION

VOCATION

Comfortable, but feeling of emptiness

What you can be **PAID FOR**

Excitement and complacency, but sense of uncertainty

Figure 5.1 Ikigai

On my thirty-sixth birthday, I made a note in my calendar for my fortieth birthday: "STOP!" I was telling my future self to stop doing what the economy and culture expected me to do and find a way to marry my passions and my skills. At the time I made the note, I was a strategy consultant—a position that had been my goal—and I loved what I was doing. The work was interesting, I was learning a lot, having a positive impact, and seeing the world. I liked my colleagues and our clients, but it wasn't my passion. I didn't know what was, but I knew what I was doing was a means to an end, not the end in itself.

Strategy consulting was great, but it wasn't something I wanted to do for the rest of my life. I wasn't passionate about it. I loved it, and I knew I was serving my passion—whatever that turned out to be—by saving up money, deepening my understanding of the world, and learning organizational design, marketing, culture development, supply chain management, and business strategy, which I was pretty sure would be useful later.

Two years later, on a beautiful, hot Houston day, I was lazing by the pool with a few friends drinking vodka-grape-juice slushies (I'm from a small town, okay). The conversation had died down when Amy mentioned an interesting tidbit she'd heard. The high blue sky opened, and a lightning bolt hit me full in the chest with her words: TRF (The Texas Renaissance Festival) was for sale.

On my first visit to the Texas Renaissance Festival, I'd gotten off a big yellow school bus on a junior high field trip, and I'd felt my soul come into my body for the first time. I know that sounds dramatic, but check this out: Thirty-five years later,

I'd never missed a season, flying back to Texas from Boston, Russia, Australia, England, China, and Germany to get there. I'm not sure why the Renaissance and Middle Ages speak to me, but everything about it—the clothes, the combat, the courtly dances, even things that don't start with "c"—feels like coming home. My college roommate once described me as "The guy who was always going to build a castle," but, somehow, the idea of my spiritual home being my place of business had never occurred to me.

When my friend said that TRF was for sale, two entirely separate worlds came together for me in a thunderclap. TRF was a *business*. It had a profit and loss statement. Somebody owned it and was going to sell it, and somebody else would own it. And that someone could be *me*.

It wasn't.

I was, after all, a professional strategist, so the financial decision had to be sound, and the books had to balance, but it was still a few years away from my fortieth birthday, so there was time. I ended up walking away from TRF and another near-purchase of a ren faire before my business partner and I built Sherwood Forest Faire just outside of Austin, Texas. The decision was made that day by the pool: I was going to own a ren faire. It was just a matter of time. We opened the faire for the first season in February 2010. I was forty years old.

What Passion Is

In the Ikigai framework, there's a "What Do You Love?" circle, which, where it intersects with the "What Are You Good

At?" circle, forms a lozenge of passion. I think this points to an important distinction between "love" and "passion," but I don't think skill is really what makes the difference. Passion is hard to define but easy to spot. And it's a little bit like being in love: You can't necessarily explain it, but when it's real, there's no doubt in your mind.

Passion is its own purpose. It's not something you do in order to do, have, or be anything else. It's intrinsically reward-ing. You don't pursue it for the money or the status. You'd do it for free and if no one was watching. It may produce a product or result as an outcome, but you're in it for the process. (If you remember, this was also our working definition of "play.")

Passion is your purpose. There's a sense of destiny about passion—the feeling that this is what you were put here to do, even if you don't believe in a put-er. I know this sounds contradictory coming from a book about picking your path, but a true passion often has a sense of vocation about it in the original sense of the word—from the Latin *vocare*, "to call" the same root of "vocal" and "advocate." It's something that calls to you or to which you feel called. And when you go, it feels like home.

Passion is more *who* than *what*. I am a ren faire guy. I did strategy consulting. A passion speaks to—or comes from—your sense of self. It feels like part of your identity, as if it's stitched up with your bones and thoughts. (This is why there are a lot more actors who wait tables than waiters who play Hamlet.) It's also the reason that I find the question, "Who do you want to be?" much more compelling than, "What do you want to do?"

Passion endures. I'm not sure whether a true passion always lasts forever, but it isn't "just for now." It's something you can happily see yourself doing for the rest of your life.

Passion may not be obvious or immediate. If you're thinking, *Sounds great, George. Lucky you. But I don't know what I'm passionate about*, I want to remind you that I didn't either until I was creeping up on my fortieth birthday. In *Grit*, Angela Duckworth calls discovering what you're passionate about "a full-contact sport." Most of the people she interviewed for the book spent the early years of their working lives exploring different interests. The work that they eventually came to see as their passion or calling wasn't recognizable as such at first sight.

For many, as it was for me, the *Of course, that's what I was always meant to do!* is only obvious in retrospect. So, if you don't know what you're passionate about, don't worry! We have action items coming up that will help you find or create your own. Passion is something you can and should be intentional about. Because it matters.

Why Passion Matters

One of my favorite thinkers today is Scott Galloway. He's a professor at the New York Stern School of Business. I really love his books, *The Algebra of Happiness* and *Adrift: America in 100 Charts*. However, his framework for choosing a career is pretty much Ikigai after deleting the Passion circle. He goes so far as to say that "passion is bullshit." Here is his framework:

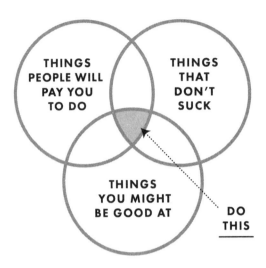

Figure 5.2 Galloway framework

Galloway's argument is that if you find something you're good at and work your butt off to get great at it, then the passion will come. Well, maybe, maybe not. Seems to me deleting the passion circle is nuts. I think Scott needs to meet more Circuit Rennies.* They chose to follow their passion early on, and while they typically aren't financially rich, many are truly flourishing!

While it can be difficult to quantify things like passion and happiness, it hasn't stopped some scientists from trying and other scientists from aggregating those efforts into a meta-analysis of adults working across a range of fields. The results are pretty clear. Having a passion makes you happier

---

* "Circuit Rennies" are people who travel the country year-round performing or vending at Renaissance festivals. They're jousters, musicians, jugglers, boot makers, glass blowers, painters, and much, much more!

and more productive. Doing work that aligns with your passion significantly increases your job satisfaction, which equally dramatically impacts your overall happiness. Workers whose careers match their passion do their jobs better and stay in them longer, and students whose passions match their studies drop out less frequently and earn higher grades.[1]

There's also a positive feedback loop between passion and persistence. You're more willing to stick with a passion because it's intrinsically rewarding and part of who you are. Sticking with something, even when it's hard, increases your enjoyment of it. In fact, Angela Duckworth defines "grit" (which she claims, "predicts achievement in really challenging and personally meaningful contexts") as "passion and perseverance for long-term goals." In other words, passion matters because, with it, you're more likely to get more of what matters to you most.

In a survey I conducted for this book, which you can find on my website,[†] a bit more than two-thirds of respondents knew what they were passionate about.

Do you know what you're passionate about?

Figure 5.3 Survey 1

---

†   https://www.georgeappling.com/book-and-speaking

HOW TO GET STRUCK BY LIGHTNING

First, get yourself a pool, some grape juice, and vodka (if that's legal). It probably won't help you discover your passion, but it makes for a nice afternoon. The more broadly generalizable part of my experience is both simpler and subtler. Because I intended to quit my job and do something I was passionate about when I turned forty, I was on the alert for what that something might be. I wasn't on a quest to find myself. I was actively constructing a great life, working a job I loved, saving money, and racking up skills. And I was keeping an eye out. I didn't step off that school bus in junior high and decide I was going to own a ren faire one day. It was one of many things I loved doing, but it wasn't a passion until much later when something I'd done for decades came together with a bit of timely information and—boom!

So the first step is exposure. You won't get hit by lightning if you never leave the house.

EXPOSE YOURSELF

"One of the huge mistakes people make," Jeff Bezos, founder of the wildly successful online behemoth Amazon, has said, "is that they try to force an interest on themselves without experimenting." Get out into your life and put yourself in the way of the widest possible variety of experiences. The best may point you toward a passion; the worst will give you stories to tell.

My friend Graham is a four-time national champion Scottish Harp player and a diesel mechanic. If I asked you to guess which is his passion, I bet you'd get it wrong. Graham grew up traveling the country playing music with his parents and three siblings and at twenty discovered his passion for engine repair. I'd guess there are about as many harpists who experiment with engines as there are diesel mechanics who experiment with the harp, but Graham didn't buy into the stereotypes of either and found something that he's truly passionate about.

When I went off to college, I already had my career path roughly mapped out, and I knew it started with a business degree. My dad's advice was to take one extra accounting course each semester and graduate in three years. As an example of why we all need mentors, I got some much better advice from Jay Wayne Stark. He was Texas A&M's version of the old man on the mountain. Already retired by the time I got there, he still maintained an office on campus to which he occasionally summoned select students.

You didn't just drop by J. Wayne Stark's office. You waited to be called. If you were lucky, after a few 4.0 semesters, he'd send someone to tap you on the shoulder and deliver the news, "Mr. Stark wants to see you." I can still feel the thrill of honor I felt at those words.

When I met with him, he gave me the best advice I got in my four years of college. "Look here, young man," he told me. "You're studying business. That's a useful degree. Do that. But you're doing it here, at this university where we have world-class faculty in dozens of fields, so take your business classes, but take these twenty others, too."

So I took courses in Shakespeare, metaphysics, global

politics, the philosophy of art, astronomy, medieval history (shocker!), and more.

"Don't kid yourself that you'll do it later," he said. "No one ever does it later. Do it now."

So I did. I took the courses on his list, and then I took others just because they looked interesting. I ended up graduating—not in three years as Dad had recommended, not even in the standard four—but in five years and with two degrees.

If you're not sure what your passions are, deliberately expose yourself to lives, careers, and pursuits well outside of whatever you grew up with. Think broadly, stay open-minded, and pay attention to the little sparks of interest that might signal a whole electrical storm of passion twenty years in the future. Here's how to start:

Pick Your Passion

By the end of this chapter, you're going to have a list of three things that you think you might be passionate about one day. I've provided two ways of uncovering things that might go on that list—one mines the past and the other maps your present interests. How you get there is up to you. I can already hear some of you thinking, "If I already know what I'm passionate about, can I skip the rest of this chapter?"

You can do anything you want. This is your life you're building. But I'd recommend doing the work of adding two possible passions to the one you're sure about, not because I think you're wrong or to make you second-guess yourself or test your resolve, but because one of the hallmarks of passion is a *density of loves.*

I love acting. I love courtly dancing. I love sword fighting. I love horse riding. I love entertaining people. I love music. I love artisanship. I love making people smile. I love drinking mead. Had I never gone to a ren faire, I might well have found my passion in the theater, but I might never have gotten on a horse. I get to do almost everything I love every day of the faire.

MINE THE PAST

In *Positive Intelligence*, Shirzad Chamine recommends tacking a photo of your five-year-old self to the wall as an empathy prompt. There's an interesting corollary between the child and the sage self, between the most innocent and the wisest versions of a self. In part, I think, it's because both are authentic. The cognitive distortions and mental saboteurs either haven't kicked in or have been transcended, and passion comes easily to both.

TAKE ACTION MINING THE PAST FOR PASSION

1. Think back to your childhood. Did you have a passion? What was it? (e.g., a sport, an animal, a cause, an area of interest?)

_____

_____

_____

_____

2. What features did your favorite forms of—screen-free—
play have? Did you like to play outside or inside? Building
games, make-believe games, or puzzle-solving? Did they
include a fantasy, social, or entrepreneurial element? Was
there a kind of play you didn't like? Why not?

_____

_____

_____

_____

_____

_____

3. When well-meaning, if misguided, adults asked you what
you wanted to do when you grew up, how did you answer?
When left on your own, how did you entertain yourself?
What were your favorite kinds of play?

_____

_____

_____

_____

_____

_____

4. Do any of these suggest a passion? Is there a theme that unites them?

_____

_____

_____

_____

THE BEST BAD DAY

It was fifteen minutes before the usual 10:00 a.m. opening at the faire, and the cast was gathered just inside the gate, ready to launch into the little skit that starts the day, when one of the actors pointed skyward. We all looked up and saw the thin gray clouds that often skim a February morning in Texas moving with unusual speed. They were darkening too, mounding up on each other like ash under a fire.

The temperature dropped twenty degrees in five minutes. We did our skit, the opening cannon went off, the gates opened, and everyone in the cast ran to add a layer or two to their costumes. Ten minutes later, the cold front we'd watched building arrived. The cloud bank rolled over the faire ground palisades like a swarming army. The temperature had dropped to twenty-eight degrees. Then it started sleeting.

There were fewer than two hundred patrons with more unlikely to come out on a day like that, and I knew the artisans weren't going to sell anything. I also knew many of them lived in nearby towns and would want to get home before the roads got worse. Maybe it was just because I've read medieval fantasy and history books my whole life, but between the cold and the people in garb, I was reminded of the Christmas feasts I'd read about. I'd always found them moving—a king providing warmth and food for his people and everyone coming together to celebrate when the days were dark and cold. So I sent my operations team through the village and told everyone that the faire was going to close, but the great hall was open and heated and that anyone who wanted to could come and enjoy themselves.

We opened a bar in the corner and brought in the entertainers one after the other to perform for each other and the 175 patrons who stayed. Everyone was in costume, the vendors who lived onsite came in and sold their wares, and the turkey leg guy walked around selling turkey legs. It was raucous and unplanned and felt like what I imagine a real medieval Christmas party would have been like but with flushing toilets and no lice. Everyone threw themselves into the spirit of the thing and had the best faire day ever. The weather was awful, and, financially, it was a terrible day, but I loved every minute of it.

TAKE ACTION ON YOUR BEST BAD DAY

Think about the times in your life when something went wrong and it was still great. Who were you with? What were you doing? What elements have turned a bad experience into a good one in your life?

Think about a time when something went wrong and it

wasn't great. Put on your silver lining glasses and look for the good that came out of it. What are the things that matter to you enough that they can turn bad into good?

If you had two hours to spend in a bookstore and had to stay in just one section, which section would you choose? Think about the last time you saw a movie or read something that made you teary-eyed, angry, or energized. When was the last time you involuntarily jumped to your feet with a "Hell yeah!" and your fist in the air? Are there certain kinds of stories that always move you?[‡]

What causes do you believe in? What ideals or beliefs would you go to war for, or at least get into an argument about?

[‡] For me, it's stories of loyalty. I get choked up every time I tell the story of King Richard who, on crusade in the Holy Land, was approached by a rider with news that a nearby group of Christians was being attacked. Richard had only a small group of thirty and only half were kitted out for battle, so he sent them on to get started and promised he and the other half would follow in a few minutes.

He and the second group were on their way when one of the first fifteen came back with word that the entire thing was a set-up. There was an army waiting to slaughter him and end the Crusade.

Of course, everyone urged Richard to avoid the trap, but he wouldn't hear it. We still have his last words before riding into the incredibly uneven battle, "I sent those men there with a promise of my aid. If they should die without me, may I never again be called king!"

That he put such value on his word and on standing—and dying, if necessary—with his friends gets me every time.

Richard galloped into the enemy at full speed. Before they could register that the English king was among them, he'd plowed through their ranks to smash their leader in the chest with his lance. With their figurehead down and facing that level of lunacy, the opposing army just gave up. Richard didn't die that day, but it isn't the outcome of that story that matters to me, it's Richard's loyalty.

What principles or values is it important to you that your work not violate?

THE PASSION REFRAME

There's a famous story called the "Parable of the Bricklayer." It goes a little something like this: A traveler stumbles across a cathedral under construction. She walks up to a brick-layer and asks what he's doing. The bricklayer answers rather grudgingly, "I'm laying bricks. I have bills to pay." This brick-layer sees his work as a job—a means to an end. The end is typically paying rent.

The traveler moves to the second bricklayer and asks, "What are you doing there?" The second bricklayer says, "Well, I'm laying bricks. You see, this cathedral will take years to complete, and everyone in this city knows about it. So if I build a good reputation for quality work, I can make a living here for the rest of my life." This bricklayer sees his work as a profession—a stepping-stone to the next stage of his career.

The traveler moves to the third bricklayer and asks, "What are you doing?" The third bricklayer, eyes gleaming, says, "I'm building the house of God. This place will save thousands of souls for hundreds of years!" This bricklayer sees his work as a calling.

Amy Wrzesniewski, a psychology professor at Yale University, did a fascinating study on people who considered their work a job, career, or calling. In one study, she surveyed secretaries expecting that very few of them would identify their occupation as a calling. What she found was the percentages tracked with other populations she'd studied. Her conclusion? Almost any occupation can be a job, a career, or a calling, depending on how the person looked at the work they did. You won't be surprised to learn that Wrzesniewski also found that people who viewed their work as a calling were more successful *and* more fulfilled.[2]

For people who think of a calling as a kind of magic that exists somewhere "out there" waiting to be discovered, this doesn't make any sense. But a calling is just that: a calling. You have to *answer*. You have to take an active role in developing and deepening what may be just an interest or pleasure at the moment.

TAKE ACTION REFRAMING FOR PASSION

1. What do you do every day?

_____

_____

_____

_____

_____

_____

_____

2. What do you do only on vacation or with your best friends?

_____

_____

_____

_____

3. What do you do because you have to?

_____

_____

_____

_____

4. What do you do when you're "killing time?"[§]

_____

_____

_____

_____

[§] "As if you could kill time without injuring eternity." —Henry David Thoreau

5. Are any of these activities something you could reframe as a calling because it actually serves a higher purpose?

_____

_____

_____

_____

_____

LEVEL DOWN

In one of my early years at McKinsey, I stayed up most of the night building the supply curve of paraffin wax in the United States. I had a blast doing it. I'm not passionate about paraffin wax. I'm not even passionate about supply curves. So why did I get such a kick out of this? When I took a deeper look at my reaction to the task, I realized that I was turned on by the analytical insight it generated. I was very confident about what would happen to wax prices if any given plant went offline and what would happen when a new plant, under construction at the time, came online. That was a thrill! It's a passion that shows up in the data sets and correlations I track between our advertising spend and faire attendance, adding to the things I love about my job. Remember, a passion is often a density of loves.

Best-selling author Mark Manson tells a similar story about recognizing the principle beneath his obsession with video games which he admits to playing "instead of doing more important things like studying for an exam or showering regularly or speaking to other humans."[3]

It wasn't until he stopped gaming that he realized it wasn't the games, their stories, or graphics that he was passionate about. He had a passion for improvement, "for being good at something, and then trying to get better . . . It's the competition with others and with myself that I thrive on." He then made his passion for improvement and competition part of his business and became much more successful.

TAKE ACTION GOING A LEVEL DOWN

Go over your answers to the last few questions and look for commonalities and underlying themes—things like problem-solving or collaboration, organizing things or pursuit of mastery, teaching, investigation, or exploration.

The Passion Tree

At McKinsey, the goal in analyzing a tree like this was to be MECE (mutually exclusive, collectively exhaustive), meaning that every instance was covered but then none could belong in more than one category. That isn't our aim here. People and their passions aren't so tidily compartmentalizable. The goal here is just to get the wheels turning and the juices flowing. Don't look at the first category (people, things, world) and pick one. Follow each through the subdivisions to the examples looking not for "The Answer" but for sparks—little glimmers of excitement or curiosity that you think might be worth additional exploration or could lead somewhere rewarding. Crawl through the chart slowly, paying attention to anything that feels particularly interesting to you, and take notes about those things that seem to have a gravitational pull on you.

Passion Tree

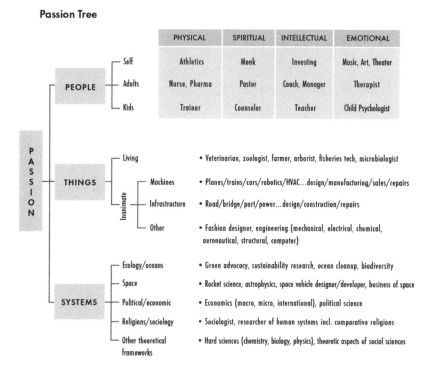

		PHYSICAL	SPIRITUAL	INTELLECTUAL	EMOTIONAL
PEOPLE	Self	Athletics	Monk	Investing	Music, Art, Theater
	Adults	Nurse, Pharma	Pastor	Coach, Manager	Therapist
	Kids	Trainer	Counselor	Teacher	Child Psychologist

PASSION

THINGS
- Living — • Veterinarian, zoologist, farmer, arborist, fisheries tech, microbiologist
- Inanimate
  - Machines — • Planes/trains/cars/robotics/HVAC…design/manufacturing/sales/repairs
  - Infrastructure — • Road/bridge/port/power…design/construction/repairs
  - Other — • Fashion designer, engineering (mechanical, electrical, chemical, aeronautical, structural, computer)

SYSTEMS
- Ecology/oceans — • Green advocacy, sustainability research, ocean cleanup, biodiversity
- Space — • Rocket science, astrophysics, space vehicle designer/developer, business of space
- Political/economic — • Economics (macro, micro, international), political science
- Religions/sociology — • Sociologist, researcher of human systems incl. comparative religions
- Other theoretical frameworks — • Hard sciences (chemistry, biology, physics), theoretic aspects of social sciences

Figure 5.4 Passion Tree

As an example, with the first category, "people," the question you should ask yourself isn't, "Am I passionate about people?" Think more broadly. What aspects of yourself and others are most interesting to you? How do you most like to interact with them? Do you feel lonely if you're not part of a team, or do other people slow you down? Are you more passionate about pushing the limits of what's possible, or about earning everything you can? Would you rather analyze people individually, like a therapist might, or collectively, the way a sociologist or political theorist does? Are you more interested in motivating and leading or helping and healing?

Or maybe you're not that into people. Ask yourself the same kind of questions about living things or inanimate ones. Does the idea of helping animals or understanding the microbiome light you up? Do you want to investigate viruses or nurture entire ecologies? Or maybe you're interested in machines. Do you love figuring out how things work or inventing new recipes? Are you interested in building or repairing buildings or machinery or programming computers?

Do ideas, theories, and systems excite you? Are you passionate about justice or beauty, philosophy or astronomy?

Another path through the chart might be asking yourself what you're most interested in serving. Do you want to serve people? What kind—children, adults, or the elderly? Those in power or the disenfranchised? Creative people or analytical ones? Or maybe you're not interested in serving people directly. Are you interested in serving ideals? Which ones? Justice? Beauty? Democracy? Environmentalism?

You can also look at the tree through the lens of value. What kind of value do you want to create? Economic or emotional? Physical or creative?

What about scale? Do you want to work on big projects that take years to complete or a wider variety of smaller ones? Do you want to work one-on-one with people, with small groups or large? Face to face or at a distance?

Do you want to know how things, people, animals, or systems work, or do you put more of a premium on getting things done, on execution, or on achievement? Would you rather work in careful detail or broad strokes? Would you rather have variation, excitement, and uncertainty or routine, predictability, and security?

NOTES

_____

_____

_____

_____

_____

_____

_____

_____

_____

_____

_____

_____

Take Action Spotting Passion

Bill Damon tells parents to keep part of their selective perception filters set to notice when their children get excited about something. Ask them about it. Are you reading it right, or is there something adjacent that really lit them up? Then help them explore the interest area. Get some books on the topic and find someone to talk to your child about it.¶

Because you're taking ownership of your life, this is now your job. Pay attention to anything that gets your energy up—anything that excites, intrigues, or angers you—and make a note of it. Remember, a passion, as we've defined it, is something you do for its own sake that you feel justifies your life and defines who you are, but which may not be immediately obvious. Or, to quote Angela Duckworth again, "Passion for your work is a little bit of discovery followed by a lot of development and then a lifetime of deepening."[4] We've been doing discovery for most of this chapter. Now it's time to do some development.

If you've taken action on the Take Action items in the "Mine the Past" and "Passion Tree" sections, you should have a list of things you might be passionate about. The "Try Something Tree" that follows will help you pick one to commit to engaging actively** for at least a year or until it reaches a natural ending point—this could mean finishing the novel you set out to write or making it to the end of the season of a new sport. It could be the completion of a business plan or the end of a course.

¶   This is the first of twelve steps of Damon's "path to purpose," which he lays out in his book by the same name.

**   Active engagement means you're putting at least five hours a week into doing more than daydreaming or watching YouTube about it.

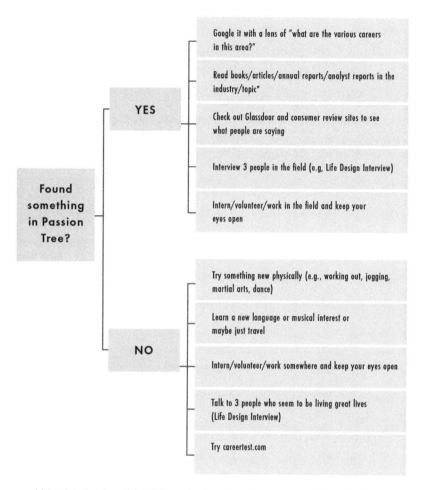

*If the industry/topic has publicly traded companies, then equity analyst reports are a good source of information.

Figure 5.5 Try Tree

Knowledge Is Capital

If you know something the world ought to know and you're passionate about it, particularly if it's both salient and emotional, you can probably get paid to teach it. Make a video, create an online course, write a how-to guide, or create a workshop. Test it on friends and improve it. If the outcome will improve social conditions, look for a charitable or governmental funding source. If not, sell it directly to the people who need it. You can offer private lessons through a platform like Thumbtack.com or TakeLessons.com or tutor people in person or online. If it is particularly compelling, you could build your own online presence and sell directly to customers. Many colleges and libraries, senior centers, and daycares offer informal, short, inexpensive community education classes in almost anything you can think of. Apply to teach your passion through one of these channels.

Finally, if there's nothing on your list that you feel excited about trying, pick one of these:

1. Learn a new language well enough to have a conversation with a native speaker, and then have that conversation—ideally in the country where it's spoken. Learning a second language will change the architecture of your brain in ways that will make you smarter for the rest of your life.

2. Learn a new sport, martial art, or another physical discipline, like dance or parkour, well enough to compete or perform. Or, finally get serious about working out and set a hard but achievable goal like a target weight (or preferably body fat percentage). Physical activity changes your brain in ways that are incredibly positive, and it improves your physical health. Vigorous physical activity is also one of the best things you can do for your brain health.

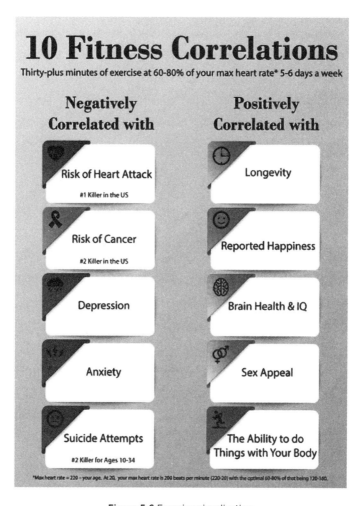

Figure 5.6 Exercise visualization

3. Learn a new musical instrument well enough to perform at least one song for at least six people, and then perform it.

4. Get any kind of job or internship. It will give you something to put on your resume and, if nothing else, give you some experience of what you don't want to do with your life.

5. Interview three people who seem to be living great lives. Say to them, "You seem to be living your best life, would you mind if I interviewed you? It's only for me, not a publication." You'll be surprised how many will say "yes." And when one says "no" that means you're one step closer to the next "yes." (See? Silver lining glasses!)

KEY TAKEAWAYS

- A passion is something you do for its own sake that justifies your life and defines who you are. Intentionally choosing a career path that aligns with a passion will increase your happiness and productivity. If you don't immediately know what you're passionate about, get intentional about finding out. Expose yourself to a wide range of ideas, people, and fields. Mine your past and reframe your passion. Then pick something to try and take action!

- If you do, not only will you have proven to yourself that you can take ownership of your life, you'll have also built grit and added at least one new skill to your arsenal, whether or not it's something you've grown passionate about.

CHAPTER 6

What Are You Good At?

IKIGAI

A Japanese concept meaning "a reason for being"

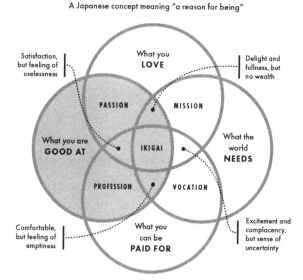

Satisfaction, but feeling of uselessness

Delight and fullness, but no wealth

What you LOVE

PASSION

MISSION

What you are GOOD AT

IKIGAI

What the world NEEDS

PROFESSION

VOCATION

Comfortable, but feeling of emptiness

What you can be PAID FOR

Excitement and complacency, but sense of uncertainty

Figure 6.1 Ikigai

Passion isn't enough. No matter how much you love something, if you're terrible at it or temperamentally ill-suited to it, you're not going to experience mastery or even competency, which is one of the fundamental needs of human flourishing, so the next question we need to ask is: What are you good at?

I WORSHIP AT THE ALTAR OF COMPETENCE. That brings us to the second circle in the Ikigai framework, which asks you to assess what you're good at. I always found that maddeningly vague. Assessing your own strengths isn't easy. About half the people I know think they're great at everything. The other half aren't sure they're good at anything at all. But it's an important part of the framework and a critical thing to know about yourself. Passion is great, but competence trumps everything.

Of course, nobody's good at anything worthwhile the first time they give it a try—which is why grit is so important—but it makes sense to play to your strengths, and that's a lot harder to do if you don't know what they are. I'm going to provide you with some online assessment tools that you can use to get a more objective look at your abilities, but first, I want to explain my framework for doing your own subjective evaluation of what you do well and talk a little bit about the key differences between what you're passionate about and what you do well.

In the last chapter, "What Are You Passionate About?," I said one of the differences between something you enjoy and a true passion or calling is how stable it is over time. Being a dad is a true calling for me. I always knew I wanted to be a parent, and it's still one of the things that brings me the most happiness (and, to be fair, the most aggravation) day-to-day. What you're good at, on the other hand, will change over time. Some things that come easily to you now may get harder as you get older. Some skills you're lacking now will naturally develop as you age. Others, you'll have to work at.

Of the four Ikigai circles, what you're good at is the one you have the most control over. Talent is great, and you'll certainly want to include yours in your inventory, but it's never the whole story. No matter how naturally good at something a person is, the people who are best at it are always those with talent, training, and perseverance.[*]

A good inventory of your abilities will help you decide where you can capitalize on a strength or strengthen a weakness, but nobody's good at everything, so part of the exercise will also be about recognizing what you're never going to be great at. Then, you can look for ways to scaffold the weakness, work around it, or find work that doesn't require you to regularly do something you're bad at. If you have a deep passion for a subject, going to graduate school to become an expert might look great. But if you hate standing up in front of a group of folks and talking about that subject, and your career path after school is to become a professor, you're going to have a problem.

---

[*] If you think talent is destiny, go listen to Harry Styles and Ed Sheeran when they were fifteen years old. Even Ed admits he was awful and only developed his skill through intense practice and perseverance.

It's hard to be joyful in your work if you're terrible at it. Bill Burnett and Dave Evans, in their excellent book *Designing Your Life*, answer the question "What makes work fun?" this way: "Work is fun when you are actually leaning into your strengths and are deeply engaged and energized by what you're doing."[1] We talked about energy as a metric in passion-finding in Chapter 5, "What Are You Passionate About?" Here, we'll zero in on those strengths you'll enjoy leaning into.[†]

The Consulting Company Capability Set

As you've probably already guessed, I love systems and elegant codifications. That's what I'm doing here, after all—creating a career-finding system. It's also part of why I enjoyed working in strategy consulting for companies like McKinsey and Booz as much as I did. These firms have systems and metrics for everything, including the people who work for them. The framework was job-specific and allowed for people like me to be ranked by their bosses on fifteen to twenty skills along a continuum of performance. It dictated the structure of the annual performance review, which dictated the size of your raise. It's a thing every company should have, yet few do. I loved it.

As a consultant, my capability matrix included skills like

[†] In their chapter on wayfinding, Burnett and Evans advocate keeping a daily activity log for a minimum of three weeks to track when you're most engaged and what you're learning. If you have the time, I recommend giving it a try!

verbal communication, written communication, synthesis,[‡] and interfacing with clients.[§] You don't need a matrix for this, but anticipating what the capability sets of different jobs you're interested in might look like will help you evaluate how good a fit they might be and identify skills you'll need to develop.

See Appendix A for the capability sets I put together for an entry-level architect, eldercare nurse, HVAC tech, digital marketer, sports photographer, and green tech engineer. These aren't super-scientific, research-backed sets of capabilities. I simply Googled "What skill do I need to be a [job title]." I then went over to Indeed and searched for job openings for each and added the skills listed in three postings to my list. Finally, I eliminated any that *weren't* duplicates so any skill named was on the necessary list for at least two sources.

Capability sets are great, but they're better suited to jobs than to people. Happily, there's already a tool that's custom-designed for breaking relevant categories of skills and abilities down and assigning them a point value—the RPG (role playing game) character sheet. Are you ready? It's time to roll up a you!

[‡]   Synthesis is the skill of putting together elements and information from different sources to create a complete picture. It's a bit like idea algebra and sounds like, "Well, if we know Fact A is true because we read it in *The Economist*, and we know Fact B is true because the CEO said it, and we know that Fact C is true because I saw that in the supply chain report, and if those three things are true, then Z must also be true and that's a big deal because nobody sees it coming."

[§]   "Interfacing with clients" is business-speak for being easy to get along with. I knew I enjoyed people, but I didn't realize until I got into the business world how much "soft skills" matter. Like most things, they can be learned and improved with practice, but a future medical doctor without them will be happier and more successful in the lab than at a patient's bedside.

The classic Dungeons & Dragons character sheet attributes are strength, intelligence, wisdom, constitution, dexterity, and charisma, and are 50 percent physical. That makes sense in a combat-centric game, but how strong, hearty, and agile you are probably won't have much bearing on your career. By all means be physically fit, but unless you're going to fight people with swords as much as I do, the OCEAN or "Big Five" character attributes make the basis for a more work-appropriate character sheet.[1]

The OCEAN Assessment

OCEAN is an acronym that stands for openness (to experience), conscientiousness, extroversion, agreeableness, and neuroticism. Your score with respect to these five traits can give you valuable insight into your character, skills, and abilities.

Openness to experience measures how comfortable you are with uncertainty. People who score high on openness are inventive and curious, but they're often also impatient and bore easily. People with low openness scores are more cautious and methodical, but they can be hidebound and resistant to change. A high openness score would be a negative for an accountant but vital for an entrepreneur.

Conscientiousness is a measure of how responsible a person

---

[1]   The OCEAN personality trait assessment is a widely respected, scientifically validated metric for determining how a person rates on what it claims are the five most salient areas of personality with each area described as a continuum between two opposing traits. You can take an assessment for free here: https://openpsychometrics. org/tests/IPIP-BFFM/.

feels, and thus often *is*. If you hate to miss deadlines, always get good grades, feel guilty when you don't follow the rules, and tend toward perfectionism, you'll likely score high here. Conscientious people are often efficient and organized, but not necessarily naturally that way. Free spirits are on the opposite end of this scale. They're spontaneous and generous, but they can be careless, undependable, and have poor attention to detail. A high score in conscientiousness will be helpful for almost every career path but particularly those that require meeting deadlines, being on time, and paying attention to detail. Although a lack of rule-following can be a positive attribute, people with low conscientiousness scores should look for ways to increase and compensate for their lack of self-discipline.

Extroversion is the most familiar of the Big Five traits. Extroverts tend to be energetic, outgoing, people-people who gain energy from crowds, yet they can also be domineering and sometimes act first and think later. Introverts, by contrast, may enjoy being around other people, especially in small groups, but they recharge in solitude. They're more reserved, thoughtful, and careful than their more gregarious counterparts. Jobs that require you to work with large groups or speak in public will be taxing for introverts, while jobs done in isolation will be hard on extroverts.

Agreeable people are eager to get along. They're empathetic and compassionate, often conflict-avoidant, and will sometimes compromise their integrity or self-interest for their need to be liked. People at the opposite end of this spectrum are more antagonistic than empathetic and are much more likely to hurt people's feelings. They're less intuitive, more clear-eyed, and apt to be prickly. Many CEOs test a bit low on agreeableness because they're less concerned with bruising people's feelings on their climb to the top, while agreeableness creates great team players. Importantly, being at either extreme of this dimension tends not to go well. Extremely agreeable people tend to get walked on and taken advantage of. People who score very low in agreeableness just suck.

Neuroticism is the only overtly negative trait in the profile, but identifying it in yourself is less about making a value judgment than recognizing an underlying sensitivity. Neuroticism is contrasted against emotional stability and includes anxiety, depression, low self-confidence, vulnerability to stress, and an external locus of control. People who score low on neuroticism are optimistic, confident, and have a strong sense of self-efficacy. They know that even if they'd scored high on neuroticism, it's something they could change.

It can be very hard to see yourself accurately. We're all likely to overrate our abilities in some areas and underrate them in others. Interestingly, this is another place where having a growth mindset (see Chapter 3, "Being Intentional") comes in handy. According to Dweck, "Studies show that people are terrible at estimating their abilities . . . Sure, we found people greatly misestimated their performance and their ability. *But it was those with the fixed mindset who accounted for almost all the inaccuracy.* The people with the growth mindset were amazingly accurate."[2] (Emphasis original.)

Hopefully, you have a great growth mindset and see yourself with perfect accuracy, but, just in case, ask at least two other people to do this assessment for you and see how closely your views of you align. If you get wildly discordant answers, get more data points by asking an additional person or two for their input. For bonus points, if you're feeling exceptionally brave, ask an ex-romantic partner to do the assessment for you.

To hear from a psychologist on the OCEAN model and how it relates to success, search "Jordan Peterson - You need this to achieve success" on YouTube.

The MBTI and CareerTest.com

To build out a complete career character sheet, I recommend using your OCEAN profile in tandem with the results you get from taking a Myers-Briggs Type Indicator (MBTI) and from the assessment at CareerTest.com. The MBTI categorizes people into one of sixteen different personality types based on where they fall along four personality traits, each of which exists along a continuum between opposite poles. These are: introversion and extraversion, sensing and intuition, thinking and feeling, and judging and perceiving.

The MBTI is often used by career counselors to help people identify jobs that might be a good match for their personality and preferences. Like OCEAN, your MBTI results are based entirely on your understanding of yourself, so it may be a more accurate reflection of how you see yourself than of how you actually are. But I think it's a great way of gathering more information for your career character sheet. You can take it for free at Truity.com, which also has a handy tool matching type to careers.[3]

CareerTest.com takes only about fifteen minutes, and the results are quite impressive. Unfortunately, it isn't free. The last time I did it, it was ten dollars. I think it's worth it.

I've gone through this OCEAN and CareerTest.com

combination with a few people, and they've always found it instructive. One friend of mine who's been a professional writer for over ten years was surprised to find that her test results came back with college professor as the top pick and writer only third. Reflecting on that in combination with her OCEAN profile, she agreed with the assessment. She's more extroverted than most writers, and while she's found ways to manage that aspect of her career by working collaboratively on books, she thinks she would have enjoyed the showmanship of teaching. She said that had she seen both results ten years ago, she probably would have doubled down on her original plan to get a PhD rather than stopping with her master's.

Take Action

Take the OCEAN, MBTI, and CareerTest.com assessments and combine the outcomes to create a sketch of your strengths and the careers they intersect with.

KEY TAKEAWAYS

- Determining what you're good at requires getting an objective big-picture view of yourself.

- You can build an excellent Career Character Sheet for yourself by combining an OCEAN and MBTI assessment with your results from CareerTest.com.

CHAPTER 7

What Can (or Could) You Get Paid to Do?

IKIGAI

A Japanese concept meaning "a reason for being"

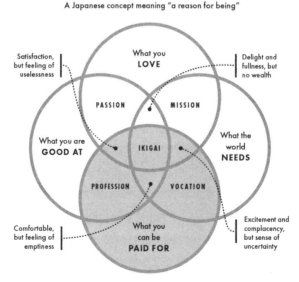

Figure 7.1 Ikigai

I agree with James Carville, who said that "all work, if honestly rendered, is worthy of respect." Sadly, respect isn't edible. Only some work is worthy of pay and, in further bad news, how much you're able to earn isn't up to you. You can decide what you'll charge but not whether anyone will be willing to pay it. The market decides.

However, understanding how the market makes that determination is worthwhile, so we'll do a quick survey of the economic principle of supply and demand, and then we'll look at the price of pay because it impacts your quality of life.

Supply and Demand

Put simply, the relationship between supply—how much of something there is—and demand—how many people want it—determines the price. Gold is expensive because there's not a lot of it, and everyone wants some. Houses are cheaper in Kansas City than in New York City because more people want to live in New York. In the labor market, this means that if you have a rare or unusual skill set that a lot of people want, you'll be able to command a higher wage than if you have a common skill set that fewer people want.

Wages at McDonald's are low because the skill set required is common. Most people can learn to run a cash register. Millions of people are qualified to do this work, and McDonald's only needs a dozen or so per store. Doctors make more than fry cooks because fewer people have medical degrees, and every-body needs a doctor.[*]

The infographic on the next page shows the highest-grow-ing jobs through 2028. Most of these jobs require advanced education, so there is a real barrier to getting into them. So if you do the work of getting the qualification, you may very well have a nice occupation waiting for you afterward.

EDUCATION

Going to school isn't the only way to acquire a skill set and prove you're qualified for a particular job, but it's probably the easiest and most widely accepted. You may have all the skills you need to work at McDonald's, but if you don't have a high school degree or GED, you don't have the qualifications. Nurses may not make as much as doctors, but they make a lot more than fry cooks (in fact, many nurses make six figures), and the entry-level qualification for nursing is only a two-year associate degree. You can easily double your earning potential in a year by finishing a community college certification program in HVAC or engine repair. As I write this, in the early days post-pandemic, truck drivers are in incredibly high demand, the supply of them is low, and the required training takes only three weeks.

It may be old fashioned, but I'm from the "most peo-ple should go to college" school. I know the arguments,

---

[*] Most musicians, artists, athletes, and many entrepreneurs make even less than McDonald's pays because these pursuits are so intrinsically rewarding that the supply exceeds demand, even for the highly skilled.

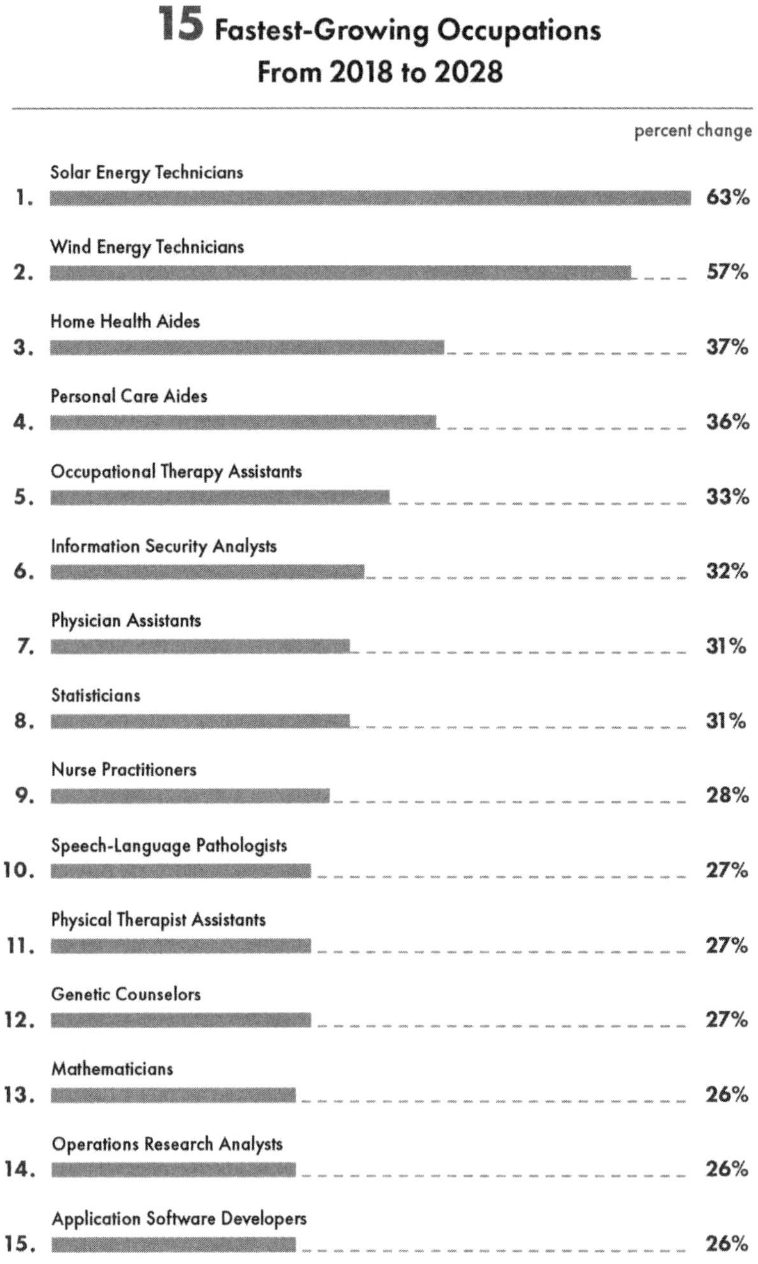

15 Fastest-Growing Occupations
From 2018 to 2028

percent change

Solar Energy Technicians
1. 63%

Wind Energy Technicians
2. 57%

Home Health Aides
3. 37%

Personal Care Aides
4. 36%

Occupational Therapy Assistants
5. 33%

Information Security Analysts
6. 32%

Physician Assistants
7. 31%

Statisticians
8. 31%

Nurse Practitioners
9. 28%

Speech-Language Pathologists
10. 27%

Physical Therapist Assistants
11. 27%

Genetic Counselors
12. 27%

Mathematicians
13. 26%

Operations Research Analysts
14. 26%

Application Software Developers
15. 26%

Figure 7.2 Fast 15

but college doesn't have to be insanely expensive, there are excellent loan programs available, and the statistics about income-earning potential are clear. College graduates earn 84 percent more over their working lifetimes than non-grads, and over a third of all US jobs require at least a BA.[1] And if you're not sure what you want to do, college is a great place to figure it out.

And college can be cheap. I've met too many young people who think a four-year degree just isn't an option for them because their parents haven't been saving for it since they were infants. But you can actually turn a profit by going to school. Tuition at most community colleges is a fraction of the annual Pell Grant award. You'll need to take some ownership and find out your local situation, but as an example, in 2022, Austin Community College costs $2,100 a year, and the Pell Grant is $6,000. This means if you took nine or twelve hours instead of the full fifteen and worked a part-time job, you could double your earning potential and still live pretty well in the meantime. Better yet, work that part-time job at Starbucks or Amazon (or any other company that has an employee-education benefit) and let them pick up half or all of your tuition.

Community colleges also have numerous training programs that only take a year. Remember Graham, the national-champion-harpist-turned-diesel-engine-mechanic? He got his engine repair certification from Houston Community College and ended the year with more money in the bank than at the beginning. Pell Grants are available for four-year university programs, two-year programs, and even one-year certificates.

Finally, when I speak to college students, I take the advice from J. Wayne Stark to a tactical level. If you really want a degree in the arts, then add a practical degree as well. That is, if you want a bachelor's in music, theater, or English, then add a fifth year and get a degree in science, engineering, or business as well. This strategy keeps far more doors open to you. I know that it can be expensive and easier to recommend than to do, but I promise you, it's worthwhile.

It's important to note that not all college degrees are created equal. *The Economist* recently published a fascinating study that shows the net positive return on undergraduate degrees in the UK and US. For both, they found that what you study matters much more than where. In fact, it shows that in the US, public universities deliver a higher return than prestigious private schools. In England, 100 percent of students who studied economics, medicine, computing, and math got a positive return on investment (RoI). Those percentages fell off from philosophy to English to agriculture with less than 50 percent of degree-earners in the creative arts realizing a positive RoI. Interestingly, only 25 percent of men who studied social care got a positive RoI whereas more than 90 percent of women did.[2]

Education doesn't have to be academic. For those who learn best by doing, apprenticeships can be a fantastic way to explore and develop your interests and abilities into something you can get paid to do. Unfortunately, the US doesn't do a great job of facilitating this kind of learning. Although 94 percent of American apprentices find work paying more than $70,000 a year upon completing their program, only three in every one thousand workers pursue this form of education, compared to 48, 33, 32, and 23 percent in Denmark, the UK, Germany, and Australia.[3]

Of course, education or training isn't the only qualification for most jobs, and it's certainly not the only thing that determines whether and how much you can get paid. A person who is very good at anything will make more than a person who's merely adequate. A qualified nurse who faints at the sight of blood is going to have trouble getting hired, even in an underserved market. To be a successful truck driver, you need not only the three-week course and certification but the ability to sit relatively still and pay attention for long periods of time. You also need to pass drug screenings. These additional factors fall into two categories: capabilities and costs.

CAPABILITY SETS

The qualifications needed to become a prison guard aren't that specialized, but prison guards make quite a bit more because the job is dangerous and demoralizing, and turnover is high—all of which keeps supply down. If you were interested in doing that kind of work, it would be important to find a prison guard or two who has a high degree of job satisfaction—who see their work as a career or calling—and interview them to find out what makes them different from the ones who quit. My guess would be that they—like EMTs and law enforcement officials—have the ability to compartmentalize. They're good at not letting the intense emotions of the people they interact with impact them.

Sales, particularly "smile and dial" telemarketing jobs, likewise has a fairly low barrier to entry, but successful sales-people advance quickly and can make literal millions. The notable bonus capability here seems to be the knack of letting near-constant rejection roll off them without leaving a residue of resentment or despair. Bartenders who perform well under pressure, ad copywriters who can produce under fierce dead-lines, and customer service representatives who can deflect misdirected rage all have capabilities that increase what they can get paid to do.

EMOTIONAL INTELLIGENCE

People skills—the ability to get along with others, to be pre-sentable, charming, interesting, and funny—have an outsized impact on income. They're over-weighted in hiring and advance-ment. Almost any job you have, get, or aspire to, will pay better the better you are at people. This isn't just my personal opinion. Ranked forty-first on the *Guardian*'s list of all-time best non-fiction books, Dale Carnegie's classic *How to Win Friends and Influence People*[4] quotes Henry Ford on this point not once, but twice, explaining, "That's so good I want to repeat it: *If there is any one secret of success, it lies in the ability to get the other person's point of view and see things from that person's angle as well as from your own.*"[†] (Emphasis original.) I'm not saying you have to

---

[†]   Later psychologists reified this concept as perspective-taking. It always reminds me of the famous F. Scott Fitzgerald quote, "The test of a first-rate intelligence is the ability to hold two opposing ideas in mind at the same time and still retain the ability to function."

acquire this capability if you don't already possess it, only that you need to be aware that being an introverted misanthrope is likely to negatively impact your earning potential.

But, if you're willing to work on it, this skill set is absolutely something you can improve on and add to your arsenal.

- Get comfortable with public speaking. There are online and community college courses on the topic or check out your local Toastmasters.

- If you scored high on introversion in your OCEAN assessment, get more practice being around people. Resolve to find some groups or clubs of people organized around something you're interested in or enjoy. This can be anything from a running group to a book club, a sports team fan club, improv class, or film society. Even if it meets monthly, the more time you spend around relative strangers the more confidence you'll build in your ability to get along with a wide range of people.

- If the issue isn't introversion but disagreeableness, you'll be better off implementing specific behavioral changes. When you meet somebody new, ask them three questions before you say anything about yourself. Notice when your Judge or Stickler saboteurs have a lot to say about the people you're with and try getting curious or compassionate instead. Check yourself for the labeling cognitive distortion and remember that nobody is just one thing. If the person you're with is bringing out your disagreeable side, actively look for aspects of them to like.

Take Action on Your Capability Sets

Look through the list you assembled in the last chapter of things you're good at and translate them into various capability sets. Experiment with unusual combinations. Are there jobs out there where the supply of people with that set of abilities is low, and the demand is high?

The Price of Pay

In the same way that prison guards make more than mall cops because the working conditions are worse, quality of life impacts income-earning potential fairly directly, if not consistently. Most of the highest-paying jobs require both a very specialized and rare combination of qualifications and capabilities and the sacrifice of any kind of work-life balance.

There are often hidden costs to high-paying jobs that are worth dragging out into the light. The first of these is stress, not because it's unique to high-paying jobs but because it's so toxic that it needs to be taken into consideration in any work-pay calculation. Previously, I mentioned that physical fitness prevents roughly everything bad. That, in large part, is because it mitigates the effects of stress, and stress causes—or at least contributes to—roughly everything bad. It will make you fat, sick, and mean. It screws up your sleep, your metabolism, your skin, and your personality. It's a contributing factor in all six leading causes of death in the US and infertility. So it's worth paying attention to.

Figure 7.3 Salary vs. Stress Graph

ADDITIONAL RESOURCES

FourPillarFreedom.com has a similar, more detailed 2x2 graph of stress and salary plotted over six hundred jobs: https://fourpillarfreedom.com/stress-vs-salary/.

Visualcapitalist.com has a terrific chart that lists the one hundred most common jobs with their median salary and ranks them by workplace quality, stress level, and growth outlook: https://www.visualcapitalist.com/wp-content/uploads/2019/04/jobs-report-ranking.jpg.

Closely related to stress but more nearly correlated with compensation is the number of hours worked. It's not unusual for people in top-paying jobs to work sixty-plus-hour weeks. I did it for a while, and I can tell you, there's a certain amount of pride in it. But I didn't have time to learn other things. I was working so hard that I didn't have time to read or watch TED Talks, and that conflicts with the value I place on learning and balance. The term for this in economics is "opportunity cost." Hours you spend at work are hours you don't spend doing other things.

Many, if not most, people in the top income bracket have sacrificed almost everything. Few are on their first marriages or have kids who like them. Huge pay packets come at a cost that you need to be aware of and choose intentionally. I'll add that strong scientific evidence suggests sacrificing everything on the altar of income doesn't make people happy.

Back in Chapter 2, "A Good Life," I said that love is one of the prerequisites for happiness and that without it, nothing else really matters. This extends to your work relationships. There's a much-repeated adage that people don't leave bad jobs, they leave bad bosses. Enjoying the company of the people you work with is more than a perk. It will substantially improve the quality of your life. When you're comparing jobs or fields, it's worth thinking about the types of people they'll put you in daily contact with. If you find artistic, creative types infuriatingly flakey, you're going to be less happy as a project manager in an advertising agency than in an engineering firm, even if the ad agency pays better.

The final hidden cost to consider isn't so much hidden as front-loaded, and it's the cost in time and money of acquiring the qualifications you need to get the job. We've already talked about education, but it's worth noting that not all education is equal. Certain career paths are much easier to get on if your bachelor's comes from an Ivy League school. I'm not saying that's a good, or even rational, measure of how qualified you'll be, only that it's the way things are, and you'll want to do some research about which schools give you what advantage in whichever fields you're thinking about. Many career paths that *don't* place a premium on degrees or certifications require some amount of dues-paying or ladder-climbing. If you need a portfolio of work, a track record of achievement, an established audience or platform, or an agent before you can get paid to do something, you need to account for how you'll support yourself while you work on these qualifications.

OTHER HIDDEN COSTS

- Location: Different cities have different costs of living and different personalities.

- Commute: An hour-long commute to work by subway gives you reading time that a half-hour drive in rush hour traffic doesn't, while working from home eliminates your commute but can be socially isolating.

- Industry-standard dress code: The professional wardrobe in some fields can be expensive to acquire and maintain.

- Insurance: Freelancing typically pays more per hour and allows for more autonomy but is less secure and typically doesn't provide health or retirement benefits.

KEY TAKEAWAYS

- Whether and how much you can get paid for doing something depends on how in-demand the requisite skills are and how many people have them.

- Higher education is one way to acquire skills and knowledge that are both valuable and rare.

- Skills, knowledge, and capabilities aren't the only things workers are compensated for with wages. Stress is personally expensive, and even high salaries aren't always enough to cover its costs with respect to health and happiness.

CHAPTER 8

What Does the World Need?

IKIGAI

A Japanese concept meaning "a reason for being"

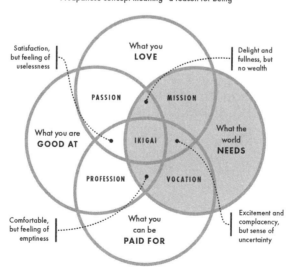

Figure 8.1 Ikigai

I loved being a strategy consultant. The work was exciting and important. It was intellectually challenging, sent me all over the world, and put me in daily contact with brilliant minds and power players. But it was never my passion. It didn't align with the value I'd always placed on being a parent and maintaining a balance of work, life, love, and play. And while the market placed a high financial value on what I did, I wasn't sure it was really what the world most needed from me.

I was spending an enormous amount of my lifeforce helping big companies get bigger and rich people get richer. Yes, I was helping people. I had a sense of purpose. But there was something just a little less than deeply fulfilling about helping only those people who were already on top, and I started wondering if maybe I shouldn't be doing more for a wider range of people.

Sherwood Forest Faire provides a day of joy for 150,000 people every year, in part because we're relatively affordable. We're even a bit countercyclical. We do just fine when the economy is doing poorly because we're cheaper than Disney or SeaWorld. (And I think we're more fun!) Sherwood is my passion, in part because it feels like a better—higher—use of my energy than helping big companies make more money. It's not that strategy consulting wasn't good for the world—it was. We helped companies be more productive and innovative and showed them how to better motivate their people, but parents who make $20,000 a year can bring their family to Sherwood, drink mead, and smile all day, and there's something really powerful about that to me.

In the next chapter, I'll make a case that if you can get

paid to do it, the world obviously needs it, but the inverse isn't necessarily true. Money doesn't equal value. Just because no one is going to pay you to paint or take care of your kids doesn't mean your art or your parenting isn't necessary. But because having a sense of purpose is one of the standard prerequisites, and because we've included having a life that "feels like it matters" as part of our definition of happiness, asking what the world needs is still a valid part of our process—with one modification: time.

Time

What the world needs changes. There isn't nearly the demand for blacksmiths that there once was—although I still know a few. In the last chapter, I mentioned two skill sets that are in high demand right now: nursing and truck driving. It's hard to imagine a future in which we won't need people who take care of other people, but will we still need human drivers twenty years from now? Not if Google and Tesla get their way.

There are fields that are clearly on the ascendency. The world is almost certainly going to need people qualified to work in:

- **Artificial intelligence (AI):** The market for AI experts is poised to explode. According to Adam Lyons of the podcast *SMART Businesses Do This*, it's going to follow the same path that social media marketing and internet presence took before it. When big companies notice a new and rapidly growing technology area, they first hire people to figure out how to do it in-house. These folks stumble around for a while and produce unimpressive results. (Think corporate websites circa 1995 or Cinnabon's utterly failed attempt at humor in the wake of actress Carrie Fisher's sudden death: "RIP Carrie Fisher, you'll always have the best buns in the galaxy."[1]) They then hire specialist agencies who know what they're doing. This practice diffuses through the marketplace to smaller companies until every plumber and baker has a website and an X (formerly known as Twitter) account built and maintained by small agencies or freelance experts. At every stage, the number of people employed first in internet and then in social media expands. AI will be no different. It will need programmers, prompt generators, engineers, consultants, marketers, technicians, salespeople, and customer service support personnel.

- **Genetic Medicine:** Since the first almost full sequencing of the human genome in 2003, scientists have been finding the genetic markers of a staggering array of diseases.[2] Even simple mail-order kits like 23andMe can now use that information to tell you whether you have a higher, average, or lower likelihood of over thirty traits, a predisposition to developing any of a variety of illnesses, and your carrier status of even more.[3] The ability to manipulate messenger RNA has led to the creation of medicines and technologies that tell genes to fire or stop firing to cure disease or improve health, while CRISPR genetic engineering allows for the direct editing of living genes. Avoiding and managing illness through genetic manipulation is going to be around for the rest of our (lengthening) lives.

- **Cybersecurity:** Data breaches are expected to cost companies more than $5 trillion a year by 2024, so people able to analyze threats to and implement protections for our vast amount of digital information are going to be in demand for as long as there are bad people in the world.[4] It's quickly becoming too expensive for even small companies not to spend at least some money on cybersecurity. Because older people are typically more susceptible to scams and hacks, an aging population also increases the need for new ways for companies to protect their customers and themselves.

- **Green Tech:** If you're smart and have a passion for the environment, you'll have no trouble getting paid to help solve a serious problem. There's an enormous amount of innovation that needs to happen in this space—and it goes well beyond finding ways to reduce our dependence on fossil fuels. We need new remediation techniques to undo some of the damage we've already done. We need to help developing countries reach our GDP per capita without doing as much damage to the environment as we did in getting here, and to help every company achieve carbon neutrality. Green tech can and must continue to make the air cleaner, the water clearer, and the grass greener and generally keep us from irreparably breaking the only planet we have.

- **Robotics:** We're already well into the realms of science fiction with injectable nanobots and part frog, part algorithm "programmable organisms."[5] Most large factories have updated Henry Ford's vision of the assembly line with massive machines snapping steel things together, and 3D printers are already spitting out everything from rockets to human body parts. Many passions might overlap with robotics in interesting ways.

- **Aerospace:** The final frontier . . . I could quote the rest of the old *Star Trek* intro voice-over, but you get the idea. It's hard not to have at least a bit of passion for the universe beyond our world. There seems to be an innate human curiosity about all frontiers and particularly this one. It's the only science that seems to elevate academics to rockstar status about once a generation (e.g., Carl Sagan, Neil deGrasse Tyson, and Brian Cox) or attract rival billionaire entrepreneurs.[6] From the obvious fields like rocket science and astrophysics to the less self-evident ones like mining, environmental design, and biology, almost anything that's being done on Earth is being researched for its possibilities in space.

- **Eldercare:** With millions of Baby Boomers retiring each year, the demand for eldercare is only going to increase, and it's already outpacing supply. This demographic of about 76 million people in the United States is going to change the health care, housing, and retail marketplace and create age-specific adaptive and assistive specializations in industrial design, fitness, transportation, fashion, and every kind of therapy. Take almost anything you're passionate about and consider how it might specialize for an aging population.

- **Mental Health:** The demand for mental health and addiction recovery services has been steadily increasing for years to the extent that 60 percent of practitioners are no longer taking new patients.[7] In 2022, more than half of the US population sought help from mental health services.[8] The only good news here is that many of these positions don't require the twelve years of higher education it takes to become a psychiatrist. Many jobs in community mental health require only a high school diploma or GED, while other counseling jobs have simple licensing requirements or certifications.[9] If you're passionate about helping people, you can get started pretty quickly and be paid fairly well.

The future will undoubtedly also need things we can't so easily foresee, which is just another way of saying that the world will always need people who have the discipline, curiosity, and grit to quickly learn new skills. Some researchers also foresee a serious shortage of tech workers, so if any of your interests lie in that direction, you can be fairly confident the world will need it.[10]

KEY TAKEAWAYS

- If the world doesn't need what you're passionate about doing, you're unlikely to be able to monetize it.

- What the world needs now is not necessarily what it will need in the future.

- Mapping what you're passionate about and good at against what the world is likely to need in the future can open up exciting possibilities.

CHAPTER 9

The 4x3 Matrix

When I was first introduced to the Ikigai framework, I loved the unusual data visualization. Overlapping circles formed elegant lozenges and triangles and made a little square right in the center where your reason for living lived. It was beautiful—but it didn't work. When we used a similar framework in my Vistage training, the instruction was to jot down ten bullet points for each of the four aspects: ten things you love doing, ten things the world needs, ten things you can get paid to do, and ten things you're good at. Then, we looked for anything that showed up on all four lists. It was interesting as an exercise, but not particularly actionable.

Additionally, the entire thing collapsed under scrutiny. If you love doing something, you're probably good at it, or will be. If the world needs it, you can probably get paid for it, but only if you're good at it. The Ikigai framework also completely fails to take time into consideration. What if there's something you're passionate about that the world needs and is willing to pay for, but you're not good at it? The growth mindset has taught us to always add a "yet" to the end of that thought, right? We need a framework that allows you time to get good at your monetizable passion or to develop a passion for something.

Finally, the businessman in me is almost insulted by the sloppiness of the "what you can get paid for" circle. I can get paid for running errands on Task Rabbit and for running a Renaissance faire on twenty-five acres. To help create an actionable life path, we need to account for *how much* you can get paid for different kinds of work and to assess how much you need to make to feel okay.

The 4x3 Matrix adds time to the Ikigai framework, collapses the distinctions between the "what you love" circle and its "passion" and "vocation" overlaps, and maps them against three different levels of financial security. Plotting yourself on the matrix requires you to be able to answer two questions: "Can you monetize a passion?" and "What is your need for financial security?"

To answer the first question, we need to go through a modified version of the Ikigai process to determine what you're passionate about, what you're good at, what you can get paid to do, and what the world needs. We'll start with passion because it's the most fun. The framework I've developed is maybe less artistic but more effective and actionable. It's a 4x3 matrix that maps the intersection of only two questions:

"Can you monetize a passion?" and "What is your need for financial security?"

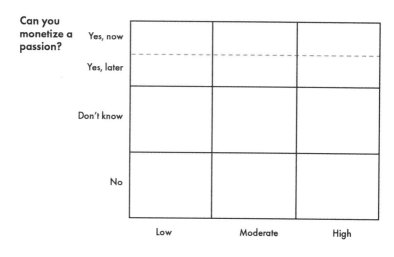

Figure 9.1 4x3 Matrix

If you've taken the recommended actions in the previous chapters, you now have all the information you need to answer the first question. This chapter will give you everything you need to answer the second.

Can You Monetize a Passion?

There are four possible answers to this question: "Yes!", "Yes, but not yet," "No," and "I don't know." My survey, which you can find at www.GeorgeAppling.com, found that a gratifyingly small percentage answered "No," while a whopping 69 percent believe they can monetize a passion either now or in the future.

With those questions in mind . . . now the big question: Can you monetize a passion?

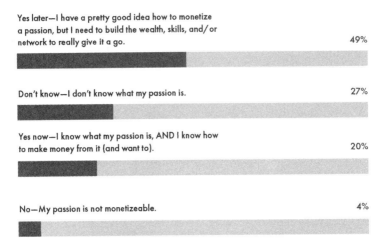

Yes later—I have a pretty good idea how to monetize
a passion, but I need to build the wealth, skills, and/or
network to really give it a go.   49%

Don't know—I don't know what my passion is.   27%

Yes now—I know what my passion is, AND I know how
to make money from it (and want to).   20%

No—My passion is not monetizeable.   4%

Figure 9.2 Survey 2

For most, the reason they weren't currently able to monetize a passion wasn't a lack of skills.

Do you have the skills to work in that field now?

YES   68%

NO   32%

Figure 9.3 Survey 3

Not having the capital, network, and reputation kept the majority from being able to start making a living doing what they loved.

Figure 9.4 Survey 4

Look over your list of possible passions and weed out any that are fundamentally and permanently non-monetizable. Don't necessarily eliminate them from your life, particularly if they're things that energize you and make you happy, but if they're things that nobody has ever done professionally and never will or if they're things you know you don't want to invest professional-development time and energy in, they're not potential career paths, and that's what we're looking for here. These are now officially hobbies.

Next, is there anything on the list that you're certain you could monetize now? Set those aside. We'll come back to them. What you're left with is a list of things you're passionate about that you might be able to monetize either now or later. If it's a long list, you might want to narrow it down. Try picking the two you think are most likely to be monetizable and the two you're most passionate about.

Create a capability set [see Chapter 7, "What Can (or Could) You Get Paid to Do?"] for each of the four possibilities and add any additional qualifications the job requires. Check it against your inventories from Chapters 5 and 6 ("What Are You Passionate About?" and "What Are You Good At?").

How much overlap is there? For those things that you'd need but don't have, can you find a way of acquiring them? Estimate how long it would take and what it might cost.

As an example, I'm passionate about history, learning, and working with young people. Being a history professor would be a way to monetize those passions. History professors need to be good at public speaking, managing interdepartmental politics, writing, and publishing. Those are all part of my capability set. They also need a PhD in history. I don't have one of those. So I can't monetize that passion in that way right now, but I could if I made a plan for getting (another) advanced degree. If I didn't make a plan to get my PhD, my potential passion for teaching history would now be a hobby.

What Is Your Need for Financial Security?

In a moment, I'm going to give you a list of ten questions to help you assess your need for financial security, but I want to share three financial thoughts with you first—two on wealth and one on savings.

WEALTH

I imagine you've heard "Money doesn't buy happiness" all your life. This is a lie. It's also an excellent example of the binary thinking cognitive distortion. Income and life satisfaction are, in fact, correlated, but only to a point. According to a famous 2010 Princeton study,[1] that point is about

$75,000 a year.[*] Beyond that, increases in income don't increase your happiness.

Grapple explicitly with how much is enough. I'm often asked why I don't buy another Renaissance festival. Yes, I could make quite a bit more money if I did so. But I don't think it's worth the trade-off to my current balance. Frankly, it's not even close. I treasure my time with my family, a moderate stress level, and time enough to focus on mental and physical fitness.

There is not an equally clear demarcation that defines wealth. The US government sets a "poverty line," but there is no "prosperity line." Scott Galloway likes to relay a story about two couples. One couple, Galloway's retired parents, bring in $58,000 a year from pensions, social security, and the interest on various investments and savings accounts. They spend $50,000 a year living exactly the way they want—including an annual cruise! They are wealthy. His friend makes $3 million a year, spends about the same, and goes to bed worried about whether there's enough in his checking account to cover this month's tuition at his kid's private school. His millions aren't wealth. He is poor.

Living below your means isn't just the definition of wealth;

---

[*] A follow-up study done in 2023 adjusted for inflation and added an interesting wrinkle. For unhappy people, additional income doesn't help over the $100,000 a year mark but happy people continue to enjoy a bump in happiness up to an annual income of $500,000, at which point it levels out. What this says to me is that money doesn't buy happiness in the absence of the more important factors we discussed earlier such as quality of relationships, perception of your work as a calling, gratitude, and physical fitness.

it's also its foundation. I'm wealthy now, in part, because I spent less than I earned and saved the rest for two decades. That's why, when I wanted to build out a full medieval village, I had the means to do so.

Remember that wealth is relative. I know very wealthy people who don't feel rich because the people they hang out with are richer than they are. Keeping up with the Joneses is a fast ride to a bad place. Take a hard look at what your basis of comparison is when you think of what it means to be wealthy.

Think seriously too about why you want the amount of money you do. Stop for a moment here and ask yourself whether money is standing in for status or prestige. As Ryan Holiday points out in his excellent book, *Ego Is the Enemy*: "Managing your ego is especially important with money. If you don't know how much you need, the default easily becomes: more."[2]

FIGHT LIKE HELL TO SPEND LESS THAN YOU MAKE. IN OTHER WORDS, SAVE.

SAVINGS

I sure hope you already know this, but in case you don't, saving and compound interest are your friends. When you are young, you can afford to let your savings ride the waves of the stock market. Over the last fifty years, the stock market has returned an average of 10 percent per year.[3] It may lose 20 percent in any given quarter or year, but over time it delivers strong returns. Now let's take a look at compound interest. Compound interest is when you earn interest on both the money you've saved *and* the interest you earn. That makes the return exponential not linear. If you save $100 per month for thirty years, at a 10 percent return per year, your account will then be worth over $200,000. Not bad, right?

If you invest $1,000 per month at a 10 percent annual return, your account will be worth over $2 million in thirty years. Think about that for a minute. If saving $1,000 per month sounds unattainable, then think again. You *can* do this.

Take Action on Your Need for Financial Security

Assess your need for financial security by rating the following questions on a ten-point scale where ten is "absolutely yes, everything you said and more" and one is "not even remotely."

		1–10
1	I intend to own a big house versus rent a small apartment.	
2	I intend to have children (the more kids the closer to 10).	
3	I intend to keep significant cash savings (e.g., one-year living expenses).	
4	I intend to go on expensive vacations.	
5	I intend for my kids to go to private school.	
6	I intend to get a new car every few years.	
7	I have expensive taste in consumer goods (liquor, clothes, jewelry, etc.).	
8	I expect to have health problems.	

9	I expect to live in a relatively expensive city (e. g., San Francisco, New York, Chicago).	
10	I expect to pay for my kid's college.	

Add up your scores.

- 65–100 is high

- 40–64 is moderate

- 10–39 is low

If you scored in the middle, you're in good company. Most of the people who took our survey did as well.

Results: Need for Financial Security (x-axis)

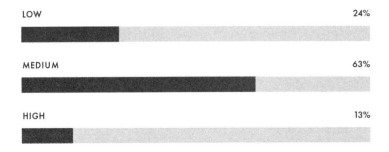

Figure 9.5 Survey 5

Locate yourself on the 4x3 Matrix by finding the box that corresponds with your answer to both questions.

There's just one path in only two scenarios ("I have an immediately monetizable passion and my need for financial

Choose Your Path; Don't Let It Choose You

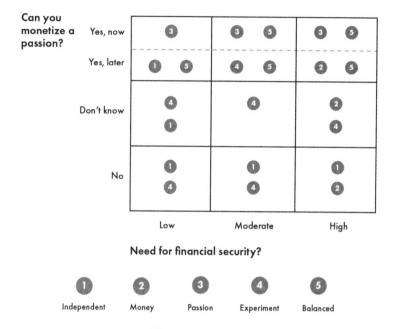

Figure 9.5 Survey 5

security is low" and "I don't know if my passion is monetizable now and my need for financial security is moderate"). For all other combinations of passion and money, there are options, and choosing between them can be tricky. There are also several scenarios in which paths overlap or fork, but broadly speaking, here's how it breaks down:

On the **Independent Path**, there's no relationship between what you're passionate about and how you make a living. Making your living will likely fund your passions on the weekends. This is the best path for people who have important non-career ambitions because, unlike most of the other paths, it doesn't require most of your energy to go into your work. You do your job, save as much money as you can, and try to fall in love, have great friends, build community, and maybe get a dog. Just keep your mind open to becoming passionate about something as you go along. Remember, too, that it's perfectly possible—maybe even likely if you believe Scott Galloway—that by working hard at something and getting good at it, you'll develop a passion for it and end up in that sweet spot of meeting your financial needs doing something you love.

You're on the **Money Path** if your need for financial security goes beyond the need to make enough money to do what you're passionate about either now, on nights and weekends, or later full time. If, when you're honest with yourself, you know that you just won't be happy if you aren't rich, or if you have no idea what I mean by "enough money," this is the path for you. This path is an option regardless of where you fall on the "passion" axis. Whether you can monetize a passion later or never, or if you don't know, if making a great deal of money isn't just your top priority, but a driving force in your life, this is the path for you.

The **Passion Path** is almost the exact inverse. Monetizing your passion is the only way you want to live. Chasing a passion is also where both the Experiment and the Balanced Paths are designed to end up. Even the Money Path can wind up here. I have a friend who went into stock analysis purely to make money and is now happily passionate about it.

On the **Experiment Path**, you hop around between fields and try out a variety of different kinds of work. If you don't know what your passion is and your need for financial security is medium or high, this is a great path to take because it exposes you to the widest range of passion-finding opportunities. Of course, there's some amount of experimentation on almost every path. Even people who are passionate about medicine and know they can monetize that passion will experiment during their hospital rotations with the different areas of specialization.

The biggest criterion for the Experiment Path, and what makes it the better choice if you're in any of the quadrants that include the Independent Path, is a high tolerance for risk. If you love change for its own sake, if you score high for openness in the OCEAN test, if you love novelty and learning, you'll be happier on this path than on the Independent one.

The **Balanced Path** is almost a hybrid of the Money and Passion Paths. On this path, you pursue financial security and build skills in the present to pursue a passion later. If you know what you're passionate about but can't yet monetize it because you don't have the capabilities, network, capital, or reputation you need to succeed, this is an ideal way to build them. This is also the path for people who know what they're passionate about but who want a high standard of living. If you're passionate about teaching high school but can't imagine life without a big house, this path allows you to have both over time.

As an example, if your need for financial security is low and you can monetize a passion later, choosing between the Independent and Balanced Paths comes down to why following the Passion Path has been deferred. Get clear about what you need to monetize your passion later and choose the path that gets you that. Do you need capital? Do you need skills? Do you need a network? Do you need a reputation?

If you need capital and you have the background and wherewithal to have a professional career, the Balanced Path is a great answer. You can work as a lawyer, strategy consultant, or CPA at ExxonMobil. Even though your need for financial security is low, if what you need to monetize a passion later is money, the Independent Path sets you up nicely to earn and save without a professional career or advanced degree. On the other hand, if you need to build an audience in order to monetize a passion, the Balanced Path will give you enough time on your nights and weekends to keep finding your people.

In our survey, this path was the most popular.

Which path will you choose?

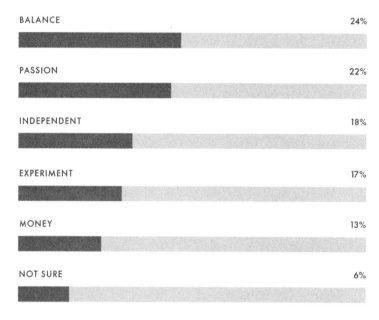

Figure 9.7 Survey 6

Take the Survey

PART THREE

Five Paths

CHAPTER 10

The Passion Path

The Passion Path

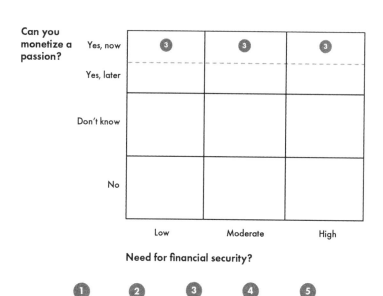

Figure 10.1 The Passion Path

When deliberately chosen, this path has a high probability of delivering a life that's both joyful and productive. It's the ultimate destination of both the Experiment and Balanced Paths and, honestly, where I hope every one of you ends up eventually. Working at your passion is a fantastic way to live. So, if you know what your passion is and your need for financial security is low, I say go for it! If, on the other hand, your need for financial security is moderate, you'll need to do some careful calculations to determine if this is the right path for you.

Preparation

It's very tempting to take off on the Passion Path with, well, *passion*. But being intentional means bringing some planning to it as well. In fact, of all the paths, this one should be the most rigorously tested against reality, which you can do by making some carefully calculated projections.

REALITY-TEST YOUR READINESS

Let's say you have developed or are developing an app that you know is monetizable, but your need for financial security is in the medium to high range. Before you set off on the Passion Path, evaluate your capability, network, capital, and reputation. For all career paths, capability is the most important (and often the most difficult) to assess. If you're not capable of playing professional football or coming up with a great app, then a wide network, plenty of capital, and the best reputation won't help. If you have the capacity to play professional football but have no real network, capital, or reputation, you can reasonably still make a go of it. However, if you want to start your own business and you're brutally honest with yourself, it's unlikely that you already have all the skills and professional contacts, enough money, and an established reputation. If you don't, you're unlikely to succeed on this path and would be much better served by taking the Balanced Path.

There's nothing saying you have to stay on it for long. Five years might be all it takes to learn enough about business and establish your professional reputation, save enough money, and meet enough people to launch your venture with wildly increased odds of success. The Passion Path can break your heart if you head down underprepared, so do a careful analysis of your ability to monetize your passion first.

REALITY-TEST YOUR TIMING

If you're trying to monetize a physical passion, timing is an obvious factor. There aren't many ballet dancers who can join a professional company after four years of college. Very few professional athletes come to the sport after working a desk job for a few years to build up their bank accounts. But timing is also an issue for entrepreneurs, even if it's a less obvious one.

Five key factors determine the success of a start-up. They are the quality of its idea, business model, team, funding, and timing. Of these, the one most correlated with success is timing.[1] If the passion you want to monetize involves taking a product or service to market, spend some time determining if the market is ready for it. I've heard myriad stories about people launching products that completely failed, only to become huge successes five years later when someone else tried.

Timing is also something to consider if the passion you're trying to monetize will be years in the making. If you have an idea for a new technology that you know will be profitable once it's completed but expect to spend ten years in prototyping and tweaking, you're going to need to determine how you'll support yourself in the interim. The same is often true for Passion Paths that require a period of dues-paying or audience-building. Overnight success is often years in the making.

REALITY-TEST YOUR EXPECTATIONS

I'm passionate about acting.

Brad Pitt is an actor.

Brad Pitt is a millionaire.

I'll make millions!

I'm passionate about my new software.

Mark Zuckerberg wrote software.

Mark Zuckerberg is a billionaire.

I'll make billions!

In other words, don't base your projections on outliers. Most actors—probably 99 percent of professional actors—are not millionaires.[2] The same is true for most artists, athletes, activists, and many entrepreneurs. There's also something called "survivor bias," which makes it dangerously easy to misjudge your odds of even moderate success. When you turn on the TV, you see only working actors. When you read books or magazine articles about entrepreneurs, you only hear the stories of the ones who succeeded. They may talk about past failures, but every story ends with success. Life isn't like that. The large majority of new companies go under in fewer than five years. I'm not saying it can't happen, but if you go into one of these fields with the secret belief that you're the exception, you're likely to be disappointed. It's hard to be happy when reality fails to meet your expectations. Go down the Passion Path expecting a low level of financial security, and then, if you are that one in a million who makes millions, you can be happily surprised.

HAPPINESS = REALITY − EXPECTATIONS

PRO TIP: STUDY FAILURE

When I decided I wanted to own a Renaissance festival, I went hunting for failures. I built a list of seventy-five Renaissance festivals that hadn't made it and dug into why. In the majority of failed faires, I found that the landowner and the business owner were different people, and that a falling out between them was at the root of the business's collapse. This made me determined to own the land on which I built my Ren Faire. And now I do, which I think is part of why it's doing so well. Investigating the failures in the space you want to inhabit not only corrects for survivor bias; it can also shine a light on pitfalls you can then avoid. Or, to quote the great philosopher Yoda: "Failure, the greatest teacher is." And I'd rather learn from other people's failures than have to suffer my own.

That said, if you truly love what you're doing enough to be okay with used cars and rental apartments, a life without much financial security can still be a stable and exciting one. If you love what you're doing, you'll never work a day in your life.

Pros of the Passion Path

Owning a ren faire, I know many people on the Passion Path who've worked steadily and supported themselves for twenty years or more. They may never build much in the way of savings, but their work lives are stable. They're probably less likely than someone in advertising or sales to lose their jobs in a company-wide RIF (reduction in force), and they're not constantly scrambling for clients the way many independent contractors in everything from computer coding to construction are.

Many of them also travel more than the people I know with more traditional jobs. My friend Roxanne has been a professional musician for twenty years, but she's intentional and good at budgeting. She'll do an eight-week stint at a ren faire and save enough of what she earns to buy a plane ticket and head over to Europe for a coupleathree weeks. She's walked the Santiago de Compostela trail in Spain and taken a bus trip through Denmark. She plans the places she wants to visit, and when she gets there, she'll put her hat on the ground and play music until she makes enough to buy dinner. Another friend of mine takes his Renaissance garb and his hammered dulcimer to Italy and makes more than a hundred euros a day playing in the city squares of Florence, Rome, or Naples.

The Passion Path can also be more reliably financially secure if your love is for the field in general rather than only for a particular role within it. I have a friend who grew up loving to ski, but he recognized he was never going to be one of that handful of athletes who makes a living on the slopes. He now runs a chain of ski equipment rental shops in Austria, skis on the weekends, and loves his life.

If you're passionate about video games and you go to school and get a degree in video game design, you work in the field you're passionate about. Microsoft recently bought Activision Blizzard for $68.7 billion, so there's money in gaming, after all! And plenty of people are well paid to work in the marijuana and alcohol industries, too, but not for smoking and drinking. In fact, you can make a decent living in almost any industry.

Most artists and athletes have managers or agents, and almost every industry hires marketing, human resources, logistics, legal, accounting, product development, project management, and sales people. If you think you could enjoy any of those roles and are sufficiently passionate about a field that working in it is enough to light you up inside, the Passion Path can deliver at least a little more financial security. Remember, most of the people who got rich in the gold rush days didn't make their money mining or panning. They made it selling pickaxes and sieves.

Passion Path Cons

Taking the Passion Path early on closes doors. If you decide to go after your dream instead of going to college, it may be harder to get an education later. If you're going deep in a highly specialized skill early in your career, you're not adding transferable skills to your resume. Spending a year pursuing your passion likely won't slow you down too much, but the longer you spend on the Passion Path, the fewer options you have. This includes both income potential and sectors of the economy. If you follow your passion for music for ten years, you're probably never going to be a doctor, lawyer, scientist, accountant, or marketing executive. It's not impossible, of course, but you've dramatically decreased the probability.

You can do almost anything you want for a year after you graduate from high school, before college, or after, and nobody will hold it against you. Walk around the Australian Outback, test yourself on the Passion Path, tend bar, and sock away some cash. But watch the clock. A year really is about all you get for free. Be rigorous about your timeline.

There's also a risk if you haven't managed your expectations for wealth creation or financial success that the Passion Path can take you into dark places. I knew a man who intentionally chose the Passion Path early in life and stayed on it for thirty years, believing that his sport would be added to the Olympics, where he would win gold and become a world champion millionaire. He's still doing what he loves, but he's miserable, and he's in and out of jail because his unreconciled desire for wealth has left him unstable and grasping.

Even if your need for financial security really is low right now, there's a risk that it will increase as you get older. Another friend of mine was a professional musician for twenty years. She traveled and toured widely and was really living the Passion Path dream. Then she had a baby. She probably could have continued doing what she was doing, but she wanted a more stable life and income for her child. So she opened a coffee shop. Maybe she'll continue to do her local ren faire, I'm sure she'll play music in her coffee shop, but she's off the Passion Path and on the Independent one. She isn't passionate about selling coffee. This isn't a sad story. She's very happy with her life and her family, but when her priorities changed, her options were more limited than they would have been had she been on one of the other paths.

If your need for financial security stays low or if your Passion Path ends up being one that also generates a solid income, there's one more danger to consider. Sometimes, doing what you love for money kills the love. No matter how much you enjoy painting, if you have to paint every day, the thing that now brings you joy can begin to feel like a chore. If you start out passionate about painting butterflies and make good money doing it, what happens if you eventually get sick of butterflies and get passionate about birds? If your bird paintings don't sell, you may still be making money doing something you love but no longer feel fulfilled by it. I know several people who could support themselves with their passion but choose not to in order to protect the love.

If your passion is a cause, pursuing work in environmentalism, social justice, poverty alleviation, or grassroots political organizing can pay the bills if your need for financial security is low or moderate. This kind of work can be tremendously meaningful but has its own risks. Progress can be excruciatingly slow and having to deal with the opposition is often demoralizing.

Equally difficult is the emotional toll of compromise. If you work for a small sustainable fashion start-up, you might be doing everything exactly right, but your footprint will be tiny. If you work for H&M and implement modest sustainability measures such as adding 5 percent organic cotton to their supply mix or boosting the wages of the garment workers in their supply chain by 5 percent, you'll have a comparatively large impact, but you'll be part of a lot of unsavory greenwashing practices. If you work as an activist or do think tank work, you can advocate for a more nearly perfect world, but likely at the cost of ever getting to see your work make a tangible difference. Finally, going into politics you might have the ability to make some real impact, but your soul might die a little bit every time you have to accept poisonous amendments to get important positive change enacted.

Path Switching

Although the Passion Path reduces your options more than any of the others, it's still possible—even advisable—to get off it under certain conditions. The Passion Path is where I want everyone to end up, but I don't buy into all the platitudes and inspirational poster sentiments that urge you to follow your dreams wherever they lead and never, never give up.

Sometimes, giving up is the smart move. At least for a little while. The problematic question, of course, is: How do you know when it's time to quit? Almost anything worth doing will hit rough patches where the going gets really hard and quitting seems inviting. Sometimes these periods come right before some kind of breakthrough. Sometimes you just keep sinking. Either way, it tends to be a very emotional time, but the trick is to get extremely rational.

Look at the situation as objectively as you can. Talk to people who aren't as personally invested to get a more distanced perspective. Then put numbers on the probability of success. Look at the trendlines of the last six to twelve months. Is this present low point at the end of a slow downward slide or a dip in an otherwise stable or upward trajectory? If there's a decent probability of success, then yes, amp yourself up on inspiration and gut it out. If the probability of success is low and you don't see the current painful phase ending anytime soon, don't fall victim to the sunk cost fallacy—i.e., continuing to put value on money already spent. And never waste a good failure. Mine it for everything it's worth.

There is a good book that is all about when to quit called *The Dip*, written by Seth Goldin. If you're going to follow your heart and try to make ends meet, please read this short book. "Never quit, never surrender" may make for a good line in a film, but in the real world, it is nonsense. If your business failed because you didn't have the right network, then you can hop onto the Balanced Path for a few years and be very intentional about figuring out what kinds of people you need to know to make it work.

Or maybe your timing was off, and your start-up failed because you were five years too early. Dig into what conditions needed to be in place and weren't yet. Then move on to the Independent Path for a while. Tinker on the weekends and work jobs that will build up your capabilities so that when the world finally catches up with your idea, you can pick up where you were and take off.

If your Passion Path is uncertain from the outset, you might want to keep your options open and go into it with a Plan B.* If you know what your passion is but you have no idea whether or not you can monetize it, sometimes the best

---

* Keeping your options open can mean anything from taking one community college class a year while you pursue your passion full time or simply keeping in touch with the professional or academic network you've already established. Even if you're not getting onto the Passion Path with a Plan B, it can still be a good idea to keep your options open.

way to find out is to try. Give yourself a time limit—not less than two years and not more than five—to go full-tilt down the Passion Path with clearly defined metrics for what constitutes success. If, at the end of your predetermined time, you've met your predetermined conditions, great! Congratulations, you're making a living doing what you're passionate about. If not, activate your Plan B.

"B" is for Balanced. On this path, you can pursue a vocation or profession that supports you financially while you fill in whatever gaps you've identified and build capital for your return to the Passion Path.

Take Action

If you're considering heading off down the Passion Path, you can go with my blessing if you complete this two-item action list first.

1. Interview at least three people who are currently supporting themselves by monetizing the same passion. Ask each of them:

    -   How productive and joyful are you overall?

    -   Are you still passionate about what you do?

    -   If you had the choice to make again, what if anything would you do differently?

    -   What do you wish you'd known when you were where I am now?

- Do you know anyone who started down this path and failed or quit?[†]

2. Create a Business Plan.

Writing a business plan may sound scary, but it isn't hard. It really is a terrific exercise and will significantly increase both your confidence and your probability of success. It is also key for start-up fundraising. There are many free business plan templates on the web. Just Google "free business plan template." Some of the key components are:

a. An executive summary

b. What problem you are solving and for whom

c. How your product or service solves the problem

d. How big the market is and how much revenue you can realistically achieve over the next five years

e. Who the competitors are and why you can succeed despite them

f. Who your team is and why they are awesome

g. Pro-forma financial statements

[†]   Interview at least two of these people as a counterbalance to survivor bias. Five interviews may sound like a lot, but I'm confident you will get real insight from these discussions.

CHAPTER 11

The Independent Path

The Independent Path

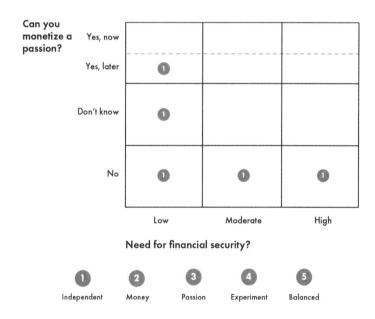

Figure 11.1 The Independent Path

My friend Nox is passionate about sword fighting. He's the captain of a troupe of sword fighters and the deputy fight director at Sherwood Forest Faire. He does both stage combat and unscripted martial combat and has his own show at Sherwood, which is a cross between a performance, a battle, and a game. It's a little like soccer with swords. He loves all of it and the tight-knit community of his fellow fighters. But there's not a lot of money in sword fighting, so he's also one of two people in Texas who can do the maintenance on a particular brand of CAT scanner. He's good at it, and it helps the world, but mostly what it does is support his sword-fighting passion and provide me with the perfect example of a great life lived on the Independent Path. Thanks, Nox!

I'd guess that most people are on the Independent Path, where what you do for a living is unrelated to your passions. Like the Money Path, there's a premium placed on maximizing your income rather than on experimenting with different options. But unlike the people who are just chasing paper, the person on the Independent Path has passions they chase after work and on the weekends. Unlike folks on the Passion Path who will probably never retire, those on the Independent Path look forward to retirement as the time when they'll finally pursue a passion full time. In the meantime, they work for money and find fulfillment in their hobby, side hustle, volunteer work, or activism.

If you're passionate about something that isn't monetizable or will never earn more than weekend craft-fair dollars, then the Independent Path may be for you. If your need for financial security is immediate and high because you had kids early or because you grew up poor, or if you simply don't want to do a monetizable passion full time, this is your path.

When you choose this path intentionally, you're not just "living for the weekend," slogging through miserable hours on the clock so you can drink your troubles away at night. You're optimizing for time spent pursuing a passion. It's perfectly possible for people on this path to genuinely love what they do for a living; they're just not passionate about it. At a minimum, try to find work that you're good at with people you like. Remember, you're going to be spending two thousand hours a year for at least twenty years working, so find something on the tolerate-to-love spectrum.

Never Hate Your Job

Be intentional about enjoying your life. If you create a plan for your life and get on a path that's making you miserable, go back to Chapter 3, "Being Intentional," and reread it. Then practice great expectations, reinforce your antifragility, take ownership, check your distortions and saboteurs, and take action.

If Amy Wrzesniewski is right, a third of the people doing your job think of it as a calling. If you can reframe your job and convince yourself of the same, you'll probably stop hating it. If you can't—if you simply can't get your head around the idea of what you're doing as anything but damaging to the world and painful to you, it's time to start planning your exit.

Take your time and be careful about it so you can still pay your rent and don't burn any bridges.

If the problem isn't really the job but your boss, you can look for other work at the same company or take a similar job with a competitor or another organization in the same sector. But if you've left your last three jobs because your boss was an asshole, you might be the asshole.

Preparation

In the next chapter, I go into detail about the highest-paying lines of work, and of these, hustling and industry are routes that people on the Independent Path can take. You can get on an executive track at a large company, rise through the ranks more slowly working forty-hour weeks, and end up as a VP making $500,000 a year with your weekends free to build motorcycles or keep trying things until you find what you're passionate about.

Many lawyers and doctors make very good money and keep reasonable hours later in their careers, although the price of entry to those professions is very high and allows little time for other things. If your need for financial security is high, you'll want to maximize your income-earning potential by taking STEM classes in high school and getting some kind of additional training, whether from a college or trade school. If your need for financial security is low to moderate and your interests and abilities lie outside the STEM fields, teaching, HR, and marketing are all great fields for people on the Independent Path.

Mindset

Remember the parable of the bricklayer from Chapter 5? How you think about what you do can have an outsized impact on your quality of life. The easiest reframe is to think about how your work impacts others. Maybe you're an accountant or a barista. Rather than thinking about your work as preparing people's taxes or lattes, reframe what you do as providing your clients with peace of mind or positive human interactions. If that's not enough to bump your perception of what you do up a notch from job to career or career to calling, find a way of directly linking your passion to your work. Consider that every tax return filed or drink made is two dollars toward your next set of golf clubs or cosplay costume.

Remember, too, that if you're getting paid to do it, the world needs it. Figure out what needs you're meeting for which people and lean into that for a sense of purpose and meaning in whatever you're doing for a paycheck. If all else fails, focus on doing whatever you do well. You can always take some measure of satisfaction and pride in having done quality work. Additionally, working to improve at anything creates a sense of accomplishment and gives you the feeling of making progress. There's truly no job that you can't work at doing better, faster, or more efficiently. Track your improvement. Gamify your work. As Scott Galloway rightly points out, the world is full of people who are passionate about jobs they started just for the money exactly because they focused on getting good at them. The better you are at what you do, the more you'll enjoy it. And, in a lovely double bonus, the more you're likely to be paid, which, if nothing else, will give you more money to spend on your passion.

If you can't find anything to enjoy about what you do, find something else. Work is too important and occupies too large a percentage of your life to be something you hate.

Path Switching

The two paths most likely to intersect with the Independent Path are the Passion Path and the Balanced Path. Let's say our imaginary accountant from a few paragraphs ago works for a large firm. He makes good money, has a nice house, supports his family, and is passionate about playing D&D. He and his wife and three other people have been in the same gaming group since they were in college. To the rest of the group, it's a fun way to socialize, but our accountant loves absolutely everything about the game.

Then one day, it hits him. He knows he'd wake up glowing every day if he had a game store. He'd sell the miniatures and tie-in novels, host gaming meetups, and carry every role-playing game he's always wanted to try. And suddenly, he's on the Balanced Path. He'll start using some of his weekend time to research what he'll need to open a game store, including how much capital and what capability set. He already knows accounting, but he doesn't know much about retail sales. Maybe he'll take a few classes at the local community college. Maybe he'll start attending sci-fi/fantasy conventions and hanging out in the game rooms. He'll start saving money and building a timeline, and in five years or ten, he'll open his store and be living the Passion Path.

People can also move from the Passion Path to the Independent Path. I have a friend who hit the Passion Path straight out of school and was well on his way to being an honest-to-God rock star when he realized he really wanted to have kids one day, so he started his own mattress company. He wasn't "selling out." He may have been a little bit heart-broken when he went from rockstar to retail, but he comes out to the Ren Faire and has a blast, and in five years, he'll sell his company, pocket a couple of million, and spend the next ten years scuba diving.

He worked very hard at the company he started and enjoyed being good at what he did, but what really happened for him was that his values (being a good parent) came into conflict with his passion for being a musician, and he had to make a difficult choice. Because he made it intentionally and has always had things that he's passionate about as a regular part of his life, he's productive and joyful—which is, after all, life's victory condition.

Pros of the Independent Path

Because the choice of career on this path is specifically made to optimize your income-earning potential against your free time, there is a decent chance that it can generate wealth over time. And while wealth may not increase your happiness, it can increase comfort. First, you can feel good about paying the bills and pulling your own weight. Second, you can fund more expensive passions, take passion-related vacations, or support people who are trying to monetize what you're passionate about.

Independent Path Cons

The biggest danger of the Independent Path lies in letting the passion piece of it fade away. Whether you're on this path because your passion isn't monetizable or because you don't yet know what your passion is, stay vigilant about pursuing it. Don't let whatever you're doing for money expand to take over your life. And don't let the comfort of wealth dull your edge. Be very intentional about keeping your passion or the search for your passion alive and hungry, or you'll find yourself unintentionally on the Money Path with its longer list of associated cons.

Take Action on the Independent Path

If you're on the Independent Path, set a calendar item once a quarter to remind yourself to check in on the state of your passion. Is it still a rich source of meaning in your life? Is it getting the time it deserves? What else can you do to cultivate your passion or passion finding?

CHAPTER 12

The Money Path

The Money Path

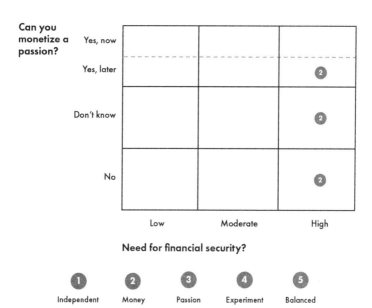

Figure 12.1 The Money Path

In 1997, at Harvard Business School, we had a history class for which the professor assigned a biography of J.P. Morgan. It was a great book, and we had an interesting discussion about it during class. As it was wrapping up, the professor looked as if something interesting had suddenly occurred to her. "You know," she pointed out, "we have several people in this class who work for companies directly descended from what J. P. Morgan built. We have an investment banker from Morgan Stanley, a commercial banker from Deutsche Morgan Grenfell, and another commercial banker from J.P. Morgan Chase. So let me ask the three of you, do you see any of James Pierpont Morgan's values still alive a hundred years later in your companies?"

The Deutsche Morgan Grenfell guy said that no, he didn't really see a direct legacy, but the woman who worked at J.P. Morgan Chase said that yes, they still talked about the company's founding values. She couldn't rattle them off from memory but said they were on a poster on the wall and probably had some impact on the company culture, but she wasn't sure. We all looked at the Morgan Stanley guy. "No," he said.

We waited for more.

"No," he said again. "We are whores for money. We will do anything for a dollar."

He wasn't ashamed or apologetic about it. He and the company he worked for had one goal and one goal only: making money and lots of it.

It's the path of many business school graduates going into Morgan Stanley or Goldman Sachs, of most hedge fund managers, and of many private equity and venture capital folks. Some entrepreneurs are in it purely for the money, as are many top executives and consultants. Of course, this isn't the only path that leads to these professions. People on the Balanced Path may work for ten or twenty years in any of these high-paying fields. The difference is the motivation behind the money. People on the Balanced Path are working high-stress, high-pay jobs so they can leave with enough money to go do what they are passionate about. Likewise, the difference between the Money and Independent Paths is the absence of passion here. People on the Independent Path pursue their passion on nights and weekends. People on this one spend their nights and weekends at the office.

People on the Money Path have only one passion—to become multimillionaires—and it doesn't matter too much to them what they need to do to make as much as they can as quickly as possible. They don't need their jobs to provide them with a larger sense of purpose, to help people, or to make the world a better place. Often, they don't need—or are willing to sacrifice—any other time-intensive interests like hobbies, physical fitness, family, and long-term relationships.

Some kids who grew up watching Mom hesitate between tomorrow's bus fare and tonight's dinner set themselves on this path. They're determined that affordability will never be the deciding factor in their lives, and they'll do whatever it takes to arrive at "money is no object." Money is safety and freedom to them; fear is their fuel.

To some other people on this path, money is a subconscious measure not just of value but of worth. They believe, whether they know it or not, that the more they have, the better they are. They're out to prove something to themselves, the world, or their dads. Money is a game—*the* game—and they're going to win. Not winning would be intolerable. Money is status and validation. It's what their ego needs to eat, and it's never full. It just inflates.

Many of the Fortune 500 CEOs and senior partners at strategy consulting firms are on this path and doing a lot of good for the world. They employ tens of thousands of people and increase the efficiency of goods production, keeping prices low for consumers. But it's also possible to make a great deal of money by meeting only two of the Ikigai criteria: doing something you can get paid for and doing it well.

Some of the highest-earning people aren't doing anything the world needs. The economy is a messy place, and it's possible to make money without creating value. I have a friend who works at an investment bank in mergers and acquisitions (M&A). Her job is to help Company A buy Company B, for which her company gets 5 percent. For a company spending a couple of billion on another company, $50 million is a rounding error, and they're happy to spend that much to have my friend's company, with its spreadsheets and smart Ivy League grads, telling them they're doing the right thing, even though 75 percent of Fortune 500 M&As destroy shareholder value. The almost comic pointlessness of what she does is starting to weigh on her. She has more money than she can spend, but her life feels barren and empty. At fifty, she's starting to think about passion-finding for the first time.

One of my closest college friends was on the Money Path for years. As long as I've known him, he's been focused on making millions. And he's done it. He's racked up many millions with questionable real value to the economy, digging into companies' financial data and predicting which ones are worth investing in. He's extraordinarily good at what he does, and he's developed a real love for the half–scientific prediction, half–entrails reading of it. He was intentional about the path he took, and he's reaped the reward—a high baseline of contentment with spikes of joy.

What It Takes

If you go down this path, expect to give up any semblance of work-life balance. You're unlikely to get to the gym five days a week. You're probably not even going to get a decent night's sleep half the time. You'll sacrifice relationships with friends and family because you're going to be putting in a minimum of sixty hours a week for twenty years. And when your work is your life, even when you do make the time to get together with people, you have nothing to talk about but work. You're not up on the latest TV shows or movies. You haven't read any books or taken any interesting trips. You don't have home improvement projects or hobbies to talk about, and even if you have kids, you're probably not current enough on their lives to be able to swap parenting stories. I've met a lot of Fortune 500 executives. As mentioned earlier, few of them are on their first marriage or have a decent relationship with their children. If I asked them, I expect some would tell me the sacrifice has been worth it. It wouldn't be to me.

I'm not going to pretend there's no such thing as racism or

sexism at this level, but I think part of the reason that there are so few women at this level is that they're simply too wise to make the kind of trade-offs that many ego-driven men make, and often later regret.

All that said, if you're really smart and really hardworking and charming enough and have the stamina, the path to being a multimillionaire is sitting right there. With a little bit of luck and a few good decisions, you can put in twenty years and end up with $3 million in the bank. The Money Path has a few different sub-paths you can go down: finance, consulting, entrepreneurship, industry, and hustling.

FINANCE

If you want to start making millions as quickly as possible and you can get a degree from one of the top-tier MBA programs, going into financial services like investment banking, private equity, venture capital, or investment management is probably the most direct path.

CONSULTING

Consulting breaks down into strategy consulting (which is what I did) for a company like McKinsey, BCG (Boston Consulting Group), Bain, or Strategy&. Then there are the systems integration and process implementation (and much more) consulting firms like PricewaterhouseCoopers, Deloitte, EY, Accenture, or KPMG. To land these jobs, you'll need to get good grades and top test scores, get into a good college, and do well there. Graduate with a BA in business or

STEM with a resume that demonstrates leadership and the ability to be interesting.* On the Money Path, you'll probably end up going back for your MBA or master's in finance or JD (law degree) once you've worked a few years, but get your employer to pay for it.

There's a high attrition rate—around 25 percent per year—for these jobs, but if you can stick it out and make partner in twenty years, you will have made, and hopefully saved, a giant pile of money. Also, five to ten years of strategy consulting prepares you to move into an executive position in industry at a much higher level than you could have had you gone into industry right out of school. Finally, the learning curve in consulting is exhilaratingly steep. The skills you learn in consulting can even serve you well as an entrepreneur—or a Passionpreneur!

INDUSTRY

Becoming an executive at a large company like General Motors, ExxonMobil, or Meta is a money-making path with three distinct feeder routes. In addition to moving onto this track from a career in consulting, you can get onto it by graduating from one of the top business schools. This will enable

---

* When top strategy consulting companies hire, they know they're acquiring people they're going to be working with for seventy or eighty hours a week, and that's just much more enjoyable if the new folks are interesting. Everyone they're looking at graduated from a great school with top grades, but if you're also a concert pianist on the side or spent every summer in Africa building houses, you're more likely to get the job, just because they know you'll have something unusual to talk about on flight layovers.

you to go straight into a six-figure position almost anywhere right out of school, but you can also take a slower but significantly less expensive direct route.

On this sub-path, you determine what industry you're going to target and then get your undergraduate degree in a relevant discipline. That could mean petroleum engineering, chemical engineering, mechanical engineering, electrical engineering, biology, or chemistry, depending on the industry. Or, it could be finance, accounting, marketing, or management, which are applicable across a wide range of industries.

Pick something for which you have an affinity, are particularly good at, and ideally enjoy. Even if you're not picking it because it's your passion, the more it ticks the same boxes, the better you'll be at it. As an example, if you happened to be really good at engineering in high school and your goal is to make as much money as possible as quickly as you (in) humanly can, you can go to college in engineering with the intention, not of working as an engineer, but of rising through the ranks as an executive in an engineering company.

Then, once you get that first job, don't be the person who leaves at 4:30 p.m. every day to go have a couple of pints with your friends. Be the person who, at 4:30 p.m., goes into their boss's office and says, "I've got extra time and energy, can you give me something else to do?" Put extra effort and additional hours into learning what other people do in the company, paying particular attention to what your boss does, and making yourself helpful to them by taking things off their to-do list and putting them on yours.

ENTREPRENEURSHIP

If you don't like the idea of working your way up through the ranks or of going to graduate school, starting your own business might look like a quick (if not easy) path to riches. It isn't. Yes, some entrepreneurs become enormously wealthy, but very few do it on their first business venture, and something like 80 percent of all new companies go bankrupt in the first five years. That means that for every new company that gets written up in the *Wall Street Journal* for doing big things or going public, there are nineteen dead bodies on the ground. Again, survivor bias ensures you don't hear those stories.

If you aren't qualified to go into finance, strategy, or one of the big consulting firms, or to rise up through the ranks in industry, you may think entrepreneurship is the best way to make the kind of money you're hoping for, but be aware, you may not actually be on this path at all. You may be taking the Passion Path and lying to yourself. Entrepreneurship is inherently risky. If making money is the only thing that really matters to you, and entrepreneurship looks like your only option, you're probably better off going the hustler route.

HUSTLING

For all the people getting rich on the well-established Money Paths, there are probably just as many blazing their own trails in the hustle economy. One of my Vistage clients is on this unmarked path and on his umpteenth hustle. He's leveraged social media to contact independently owned martial arts studios. These are all small, local one- or two-person operations run by a person who is deeply passionate about doing and teaching martial arts. That's what they love. That's what they're good at. They're not good at business. Many of them don't want to be. They do, however, want to stay afloat so they can keep doing what they love. This is where my friend comes in.

He'll gather thirty or forty of these martial arts studio owners in a room and say, "Each of you is going to give me 40 percent ownership in your company for nothing. Then I'm going to teach you how to quintuple the size of your business so that the value of your 60 percent is twice what your 100 percent share is worth right now. Here's how I'm going to do it." He tells them just enough to get them to believe him and signs them up. Then he actually teaches them how to quintuple their earnings by deploying professional operating and management systems in their businesses.

He isn't a con artist. He's a hustler. He's providing a service and adding value to the economy, but he's not passionate about martial arts. In the past, he has run a dating coaching business, a game store, and a website-hosting service hustle, and he doesn't care much about dating, gaming, or hosting any more than he cares about Taekwondo. He loves the hustle. He loves the deal. But he's in it for the money, and he's making a ton of it.

Pros of the Money Path

This path is littered with perks. You'll never have to fly a commercial airline again. You'll get front-row seats to any show you want to see. You can order the $200 champagne and wear

Gucci slippers, and you'll never lack for people who'll tell you how amazing you are, as long as you're buying.

Making, and saving, a great deal of money also keeps your options open. If you later develop a passion, you'll be well positioned to switch to the Balanced or even the Passion Path.

It's almost impossible to maximize your income-earning potential without getting extremely good at what you do. Consequently, competence, with its attendant dignity, is almost a side benefit to this path.

Money Path Cons

There's an inherent risk to the constant striving for more. If there is no end zone, there's no win. If there's no "enough," by definition, there's no contentment.

To me, the biggest risk of this path is living without passion. Even if making a great deal of money creates a life with a high baseline of contentment (and I'm not sure it can), the spikes of true joy that lift us out of our ordinary experience are almost always passion- or values-based.

Remember what I said about wealth in Chapter 9—it's a simple function of income and expenses. I know very wealthy people who don't feel wealthy because most of their friends make more than they do.

Path Switching

Because so much sacrifice is required by this path, many people burn out and switch, either intentionally or by default, to a modified Independent Path on which an anemic passion or mere pleasure-seeking occupies their nights and weekends.

I would encourage anyone on this path to at least stay open-minded about an eventual switch to the Balanced Path. If you just aren't going to feel safe until you have a few million socked away, fine. Do that. But once you do, start looking for a passion that adds joy and meaning to your life. You can experiment with different things on your occasional day off in an Independent Path model, or just set yourself on the Balanced Path by picking an end date sometime in the future when you'll quit your job and start passion-finding full time.

Take Action on the Money Path

Be very honest with yourself about why your need for financial security is so high that it excludes everything else. My guess is there's probably some underlying fear or ego trauma that you believe piles of money will solve. It probably won't. If you can dig down to the real reason for your extreme need for financial security, you have a better chance of actually meeting that need and, therefore, a better chance at a life that's productive and joyful.

SET A CALENDAR ITEM FOR TEN AND FIFTEEN YEARS IN THE FUTURE

Let's say you head down this path and go to work in some hedge fund or investment bank or private equity fund. After fifteen years, when the timer goes off, you have $5 to $10 million in the bank. The standard path is to do ten more years and make $50 million more. Instead, stop and really investigate whether you're still on a path you believe will bring you joy.

If not, consider switching over to the Balanced Path with a future end date to quit and monetize a passion. Or choose the Experiment Path and take your wealth and expertise into different fields as you search for a passion. You could even get on the Independent Path and keep doing what you're doing but with time carved out to work on a passion project, whether it's creative or charitable, athletic, or entrepreneurial.

As long as you keep being intentional about the path you're on, you'll be okay. But if you want to challenge yourself, read Po Bronson's book *What Should I Do with My Life?* It's a series of well-told portraits of people who found their way to monetizing a passion from a wild variety of different places and were universally happier for it.

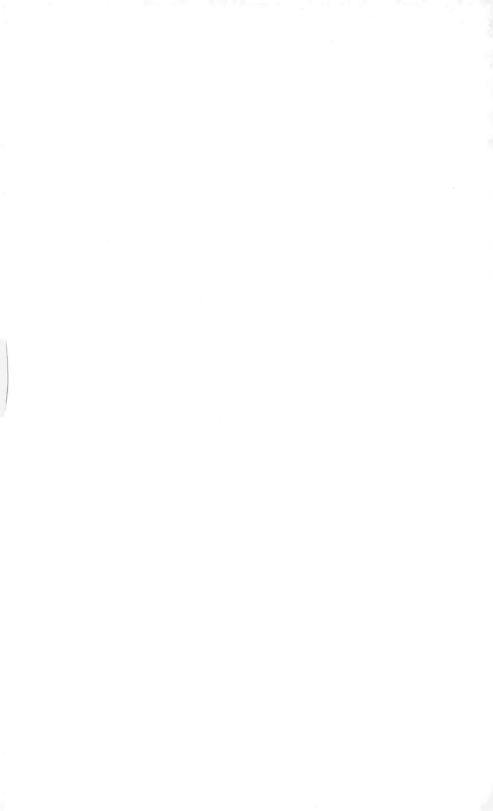

CHAPTER 13

The Experiment Path

The Experiment Path

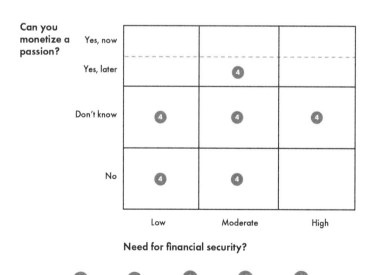

Figure 13.1 The Experiment Path

People get on the Experiment Path for a variety of reasons, all of which are worthy and legitimate if intentionally chosen. For people with a real passion for learning and exploring new things or new ventures, the Experiment Path can be a kind of Passion Path. Others get on the Experiment Path to drill down to the perfect job within an industry they're already passionate about. People also get on this path to pick up a wide range of skills and the capital they need to pursue a passion they've already identified and know they can monetize. Others don't yet know what they're passionate about and are on the Experiment Path to, well, experiment.

My favorite Experiment Path story comes from Matthew McConaughey in his autobiography *Greenlights*. He went to Australia as a young man to try things out. He writes, "I was now on my sixth job. I'd been a bank teller, a boat mechanic, a photo processor, a barrister's assistant, a construction worker, and an assistant golf pro."[1] This was clearly a formative experience for McConaughey and I'm confident he wouldn't trade it for the world.

As you can see in the graphic at the opening of the chapter, this path is an option in most squares of the matrix. Consequently, people on this path come in many varieties:

Thrill Seekers

Except, perhaps, for the Passion Path, the Experiment Path offers the highest thrill-to-drill ratio. As such, it attracts two different kinds of thrill seekers—those who want to ride learning curves the way a surfer does waves, and those hoping to get in on the ground floor of something new gambling that it will go public or sell to a private equity firm, making everybody very rich very quickly. Either way, these people are on the Experiment Path for the excitement of its uncertainties.

Surfers

In most lines of work, the rapid learning and advancement of the first few years eventually slow down. You may plateau or continue to move up the ranks more slowly, but for surfers, the point where most people start to relax is when they hop off one career trajectory and jump onto another one where, once again, they'll have to ramp up quickly. By chasing their curiosity and switching things up every few years, surfers hit steeper learning curves and meet new people more frequently.

Gamblers

Many people are drawn to the Experiment Path, particularly in the tech sector, by the possibility of getting in early on something that's going to go big. A crazy-smart friend of mine is on this path. We'd worked together at one of my consulting firms, and when I went to Brightstar (a large cell phone distribution company), he came with me as my chief of staff. He went from there out to Silicon Valley, where he hopped around between tech companies. He was definitely trying to get in on an IPO and make a ton of money, but that clearly wasn't his primary motivation. There were plenty of other options with a higher probability of wealth, but he wouldn't do it. He had seven jobs after graduating college with an average tenure of two years. He was experimenting, bouncing around, learning and having experiences, and going after whatever captured his imagination until he landed at Waymo, where he's been for five years.

Drillers

Certain companies and sectors seem to attract people for the sheer coolness factor (such as Apple or Gucci, space exploration or AI) or for their values-based appeal (such as environmental technology or social justice). For a person on the Experiment Path, what distinguishes these fields from a true monetizable passion is a lack of clarity about where they fit in. If you're passionate about working in a particular field or for a specific company where the odds of making a good living are high but don't yet know exactly what you'd love to do, the Experiment Path lets you build your resume, pay your rent, and chase your passion.

If, for example, you think Tesla is the coolest thing going, and you'd really like to work there but aren't clear on what you'd enjoy doing, first, go back to Chapter 6, "What Are You Good At?" and redo the OCEAN and CareerTest.com assessments to identify what you're good at. Competency and enjoyment are deeply linked. Then, do a little research on the supply and demand balance at Tesla for different capability sets. Are they hiring procurement and manufacturing people but drowning in branding and sales folks? Maybe they're short on chemical engineers but laying off mechanical engineers. Companies post jobs online. Go through and classify them for yourself. Identify a qualification for which their need is high and the supply low, and then go get that qualification. You might not end up being passionate about the job you get as a result, but you'll be working for your dream employer and well-positioned to reassess their needs and your capabilities to keep closing the gap.

As a very different example, let's say you're passionate about weed. You love cannabis and know you want to work in the cannabis industry. Here's what not to do: Open your own retail storefront. The marketplace is bloated with small start-ups run by stoners who don't have a business plan and haven't thought through the suite of capabilities they need to run a successful business or what they'll do once Big Tobacco enters the market. Because it will. They're already buying real estate and patents and detailing plans for how they'll dominate the industry once cannabis is legal nationwide.

Here's what to do instead: Figure out the capability set you'll need to succeed in the industry you love and go into it with a planned endgame of selling your business to RJR Nabisco or Philip Morris and becoming a million-dollar-a-year industry consultant.

Collectors

If you know what you're passionate about and believe it's monetizable once you've saved enough money and acquired the skills, experience, and social capital you need, deciding between the Experiment and the Balanced Path largely comes down to the relative weight of your financial and experiential needs. If you get bored easily or need experience with a wide, diverse range of skills and people, the Experiment Path is the right answer as long as your need for financial security is on the medium to low side. If your need for financial security is high, you can still pick up a lot of valuable skills and experience while building your reputation and your network on the Balanced Path, where there's more stability and a higher likelihood of amassing real wealth.

Hunters

If you're on this path to find your passion, you can earn a good living while exposing yourself to a lot of different jobs in different fields at different levels and in different locations. And because that exposure is done in the name of discovering or developing a passion, every new thing you try is invested with the thrill of possibility that this might be *it*. If you're experimenting in the name of passion hunting, you have a smorgasbord of options. Try:

- Working in the private sector at small, medium, and large organizations in banking, business, the arts, education, sports, and research

- Working for well-established companies and start-ups

- Working for the government at the local, state, and federal level

- Working for a nonprofit and an NGO (non-governmental organization)

- Working in countries that have markedly different geography, culture, language, climate, and standard of living than the one you grew up with

Pros of the Experiment Path

This path maximizes learning. In fact, learning is really the point of this path. If you're restless (beware the Restless Saboteur) or just find novelty energizing, changing companies or industries every few years in the name of experimentation can be very rewarding.

There's a chance that any one of your experiments might hit the jackpot.

Almost by definition, this is the most flexible path. By simply staying put, you can move from it to the Balanced, Independent, or Money Path.

This path maximizes your ability to travel widely, and often on someone else's dime.

If you leave jobs gracefully* and with consideration for

---

* A graceful exit requires careful planning. It's well worth your time to put thought into who you need to communicate what to and when. Always talk to your boss (and maybe your boss's boss) first, before you talk to your peers. Tell the truth but be thoughtful about the message you want the different people you speak with to take away from your communication with them. If your case for leaving makes sense to them, you'll go with people who are sad to lose you but happy to cheer you on. Add to that goodwill by doing everything you can not to leave them hanging—whether by finding your own replacement, making yourself available to train them, or simply leaving everything in good shape to set them up for success.

those who have to go on without you or take your place, this path offers excellent networking opportunities.

Experiment Path Cons

The Experiment Path isn't as stable as most of the others, and that lack of stability can make it difficult to sustain a long-term romantic relationship, have kids, or buy a house.

You'll probably sacrifice something in career advancement and income-earning potential by making lateral moves across companies, industries, and countries.

There's a risk with this path that you'll develop a skill set that's broad but not deep. The old "Jack of all trades, master of none" phenomenon applies. If you've had five jobs in ten years, no matter how well your skill set matches the requirements of a new job, someone in HR is going to point out you lack the loyalty gene. Skilled workers are an investment companies make, and a track record that shows you don't stick around will make them less willing to invest in you.

This is, to a certain extent, an avoidable risk. People on the Experiment Path too often miss an opportunity to get everything they want from it while mitigating the damage that can be done by a patchwork resume. If you've been with a company for two years and you're starting to get restless— maybe the probability of an IPO has dropped from 20 to 10 percent or your learning curve has flattened out—don't start packing your suitcases straight away. Start looking for something new inside your current organization. If you've been in product development for a while, instead of moving on, see if you can move over into marketing or sales, supply chain, or new business development. If you can do five different jobs, learn all the new skills, and meet all the new people within the same company, your stealth experimentation won't raise any loyalty red flags.

But perhaps the biggest risk of this path is not actually being on the path at all but drifting along on currents of non-intentionality while pretending you're experimenting.

Finally, if you're an introvert, this path can be daunting. But that might just be a good thing.

Path Switching

Even hardcore thrill junkies can want to get off the roller-coaster. If a decade or two down the Experiment Path, you find that the excitement is more irritating than enlivening, you'll be fairly well situated to switch to any other path. If you've found work you enjoy that pays well, you can stay where you are and either chase your passion on nights and weekends on the Independent Path or shift your thinking to the Balanced Path and start socking money away for a day in the future where you'll quit your job and pursue your passion full time.

My brother does extremely well as the CEO of the country's third-largest crane company, and he got there on the Experiment Path.

Mike was the captain of the football team and really passionate about the game. He played in college and had he gone pro, he would have been on the Passion Path. Instead, he became a CPA for a few years and then worked at three different B2B marketplace start-ups over several years, three of them as the CFO. He wasn't passionate about start-ups or B2B marketplaces, he was just following the opportunities, taking the positive risk for an equity bump, learning, and having fun. A smart and even-tempered guy who's good with people, he moved up through the ranks at the crane company to become its CEO. He's sold that company twice to different private equity funds and done very well for himself each time. And here's the kicker—Mike loves cranes. He's on the Passion Path now because being successful and very good at what he does has turned a job into a true calling for him.

Take Action on the Experiment Path

If you're going to take the Experiment Path, it's critical that you have a clearly stated objective. It could be to find your passion or to learn as much as you can. It might be to see the world or to build a broad professional network. The nature of your goal is less important than that you have a specific, clearly stated goal and action plan. Be exceedingly thoughtful and intentional about it. Here are some questions to consider:

• What is your goal? Be explicit.

_____

_____

_____

_____

- What actions did you take last quarter that moved you closer to that goal?

_____

_____

_____

_____

_____

_____

_____

- What, if anything, got in your way?

_____

_____

_____

_____

_____

_____

_____

_____

- What actions will you take next quarter toward your goal?

_____

_____

_____

_____

_____

_____

_____

_____

_____

- How will you judge the efficacy of your actions?

_____

_____

_____

_____

_____

_____

_____

_____

CHAPTER 14

The Balanced Path

The Balanced Path

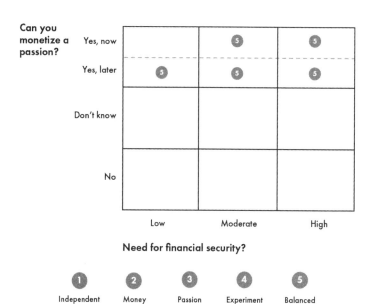

Figure 14.1 The Balanced Path

In the Ikigai framework, a vocation lies in the intersection of what the world needs and what you can get paid to do, while a profession occupies the overlap between what you're good at and what you can get paid to do. Because we've largely collapsed the needs of the world and income-generation circles, this makes skill the defining difference between a vocation and a profession. In a profession, you have to be particularly good at what you do. In a vocation, just plain good is usually good enough. As a corollary, professions tend to be more lucrative.

On the Balanced Path, you choose a profession or vocation first. Hopefully, it's something you like doing. It may even be something you love, but it isn't a passion—it's not something you want to do until you die. You get onto the Balanced Path intending to stay on it only until you've reached a particular monetary or skill target, at which point, you'll switch over to the Passion Path. Since the whole point of this path is to balance your need for financial security with doing what you're passionate about, if your need for financial security is high, you're better off choosing a professional career. If you don't have the capability set to do that, you'll need to plan to save a larger percentage of what you earn or delay your path-switching.

The key requirement of this path is that you spend less than you earn. If you can save 20 or even 10 percent of each paycheck, you'll be buying yourself the freedom to do what you love for the last half of your life. If you're working in a profession or vocation and you're not saving money, you're not on the Balanced Path. You're on the road to somewhere you haven't intentionally chosen and probably don't want to be.

At twenty, I was intentional about choosing the Balanced

Path. When I started at McKinsey, my plan was to work and learn, have some fun, see the world, and save enough of what I earned to have a million dollars in the bank by my fortieth birthday. At that point, I had an Excel spreadsheet with annual savings goals for the next fifteen years but no plans to leave the corporate world for the medieval one. I just wanted to have the financial freedom to choose. By forty, I wanted to be able to do whatever I wanted to, whether that was to stay as a McKinsey partner or take an executive position in industry or go back to school. I didn't have a passion waiting in the wings, I just wanted the increase in self-determination that comes with having enough money saved that finances aren't making the decisions. Today, I'm living exactly the life that I designed a decade later, and I intend to do it until I can't do it anymore.

While I was earning and saving, I was also getting the kind of exposure to things that are part of the hunt for passion. I worked in Moscow, Munich, New York, Denver, London, Melbourne, Shanghai, Florida, California, and many other places. It was great geographic exposure. I was also getting terrific industry and functional exposure to finance, operations, marketing, organization, and almost every other aspect of running a business.

The Balanced Path lets you have a career you enjoy, that the world needs, and that makes money while saving, planning, and exploring or cultivating a passion to which you'll devote yourself once your financial needs are covered for the rest of your life. Because it forces you to take the long view, it's great for building up the capabilities and capital that will enable any passion.

Pros of the Balanced Path

In *The Tempest*, Shakespeare's aging magician deliberately introduces obstacles to his daughter's pursuit of passion, "lest too light winning make the prize light." I think the joy I take on the Passion Path is deeper and richer because I waited to get on it. Sure, I could have started working at a ren faire straight out of college or even skipped college altogether to follow something that was more pleasure than passion. But by waiting until I was forty and had a million dollars and both academic and a real-world education in business, I was able to step onto the Passion Path of owning a ren faire rather than working for one. Don't get me wrong, it's still a lot of work, but I love every bit of it in part, I think, because it needs every bit of the experience and expertise I bring to it.

You're never going to hit forty and think, "Gee, I wish I didn't have a million dollars in the bank." A well-padded savings account is a great source of comfort and peace of mind.

Your parents, and society in general, tend to look kindly on young people who are working hard and saving money. My dad may not have understood why I didn't become the CEO of a Fortune 500 company, but he couldn't really disapprove of the way I'm living my life on the Passion Path the way he might have done if I'd gotten on it earlier.

The Balanced Path is great for passion-finding and building capabilities, wealth, and networks at the same time.

Balanced Path Cons

The first part of the Balanced Path may be harder than you think. Even if you really enjoy what you're doing, you're not getting the energy and focus boosts that come with work you're truly passionate about. While people on the Independent Path are pursuing their passions on the weekend, you'll probably be working, and while the other folks in the office on the Money Path are being fueled by their desire for money, you're there working for a future that may feel far away. Keeping good metrics that allow you to track your progress toward your long-term goals can be a huge help. My Excel spreadsheet showed me exactly how I was doing.

While it's excellent training in delayed gratification, don't stay at a job you hate just to fund your fifteen-year savings plan. I've said it before, but it bears repeating here: Never *hate* your job.

If you're on the Balanced Path to build capabilities and capital because you know what your passion is and it's monetizable, but you're not ready, you're going to be constantly asking yourself, "Am I ready now? How about *now*? Is it time to path switch, or do I need a few more years? Should I stay or should I go now?" Cue The Clash and a high stress level.

Happily, this is an easy problem to remedy. Before you even set foot on the path, define the finish line with quantifiable, unambiguous metrics. It might be getting to $400,000 in your savings account or earning your MBA plus two years of working in a related field. It could be passing your CPA exam or building a mailing list of pre-orders. What the goalposts are matters less than that they are clear and quantifiable.

You don't quit too soon because you're feeling extra smart one day, and you don't stay too long because change is scary. Set your target, don't stop until you reach it, and when you do, take the leap.

The largest risk on the Balanced Path is that you'll start spending what you earn rather than saving at least 10 percent of it. You may be on the Balanced Path, at least in part, because your need for financial security is moderate or high. Maybe you have expensive tastes or an expensive hobby, and yes, you're working very hard. It's easy to fall into the trap of rewarding yourself too generously in the present by stealing from your future fund. Don't do it!

Take Action on the Balanced Path

- Use your Capability Matrix and Character Sheet to identify the potential vocations and professions that will maximize your earning, and saving, potential.

- Create a multi-year savings plan and stick to it.

- If you know the capability set that you need to monetize a passion, choose work that will give you the appropriate experience and skills, or introduce you to the people you'll need in your network.

- If once you reach your age or income deadline, you haven't yet identified a passion to monetize, the passion-hunting techniques I detailed in Chapter 5 will work for you, too.

Conclusion

One day, early in my college career, the Intro to Accounting professor took a straw poll: "Raise your hand if you're in this class because you want to be an accountant."

Roughly nobody raised their hand.

I don't imagine this came as a surprise. The course was a requirement for business majors. He kept going. "Raise your hand if you think accounting might be useful to know for your career plans."

A few hands inched up.

Then, "Raise your hand if you just want to go to the mountains and pick berries."

Every hand raised.

Our professor shook his head sadly. I could almost hear him thinking *kids today!* I hear the same grumble today about Gen Z and Millennials: "Nobody wants to work. Everyone just wants to go to the mountains and pick berries." But what many adults forget is that being young can often be really difficult. You want to do something remarkable, but you don't know what. You're trying to figure yourself out, but your brain isn't done developing until you're in your midtwenties.

The world is a complex and noisy place full of too many options vying for your present and at odds with your future. Your parents, society, peers, and the economy all seem to be pointing you down a safe path to a certain future that doesn't look like the way to that cool life you want. But then again you're not sure what that life *would* look like and have no idea how to get there anyway. And you can't just stand still.

There were around two thousand business majors at my school on a path to becoming bankers, analysts, and marketers all of whom really just wanted to be picking berries! I remember thinking, *We've all figured out we can't just do whatever we want to for the rest of our lives. We know we need to earn a living. How can I make that a good thing? If I'm going to spend tens of thousands of hours working, how can I make it purposeful, useful, and good?*

I took the Balanced Path. I didn't have a name for it, and I hadn't scoped for myself the entire system I've since built out for you, but the logic for my choices was clear even then. I was absolutely intentional about my plan and my path based on an intuitive understanding of what became the 4x3 Matrix. I knew I had a fairly high need for financial security, and I knew I wanted to monetize a passion. I didn't know what that passion was, so I picked a path intending to make good money, learn a lot, and see the world.

I didn't name the other paths, but I did consider and reject them. I knew I could join the Peace Corps and "follow my bliss," but I also knew I wanted money. I could have gone into investment banking and made bajillions of dollars, but I didn't think what they did was so great for the world, so I didn't take that path either. I was intentional about the relationship between my career and my passion, and I credit that clarity and intentionality for the fact that I was then and am still one of the happiest people I know.

I've tested my theory beyond my own experience over the years. I've met a ton of people in a wide variety of professions and almost universally, the happiest ones are those who have been equally clear and deliberate about that foundational income-passion relationship. They may have taken any of the paths or moved from one to another. Most never have put any formal language around it. But they were all intentional about the relationship between doing something they loved and earning the rent we all must pay to live.

I've met a lot of these people, but they're still the exception. More than a century and a half ago, Thoreau said that most lives were ones of "quiet desperation." I hope that's less true now. It makes me sad that it's still true at all. But I see it every day. And I get it. It's all too easy to fall into the trap of following the well-traveled path your parents, society, or momentum has set you on.

I'm not saying that path is even necessarily the wrong one.

I'm asking you to take the time and do the work of intentionally choosing whatever path you take. Even if you don't deviate at all from your previous trajectory, you'll move along it faster and with more joy if you've chosen it intentionally, ensuring you'll make the level of income you need while doing whatever "picking berries" means to you.

The Last Page

I f you read this book without taking action, and aren't feeling the increase in joy, contentment, and productivity that I promised you'd have by the time you got here, find an accountability partner to work through the action steps, matrix, and path-picking with you.

If you've taken action on what you've read, then you've done more than increase your positive emotions. You've also become more intentional, uncovered what's most important to you, set yourself up for success, at least started to find a passion and articulate a purpose, determined what you're good at, what you can—or could—get paid to do, figured out what the world needs, discovered how your need for financial security relates to what you're passionate about, and picked the one of five career meta-paths that's best for you. Now you have a concrete next step to take on that path to intentional work.

Take it.
Don't settle.
(And get some exercise.)
And when in doubt, act.

DOING NOTHING AT ALL
VS.
MAKING SMALL CONSISTENT EFFORTS:

$$(1.00)^{365} = 1.00$$

$$(1.01)^{365} = 37.7$$

Acknowledgments

T hank you to my friends and family, particularly my partner Brian, for supporting me in this as he always has in everything.

A special thanks to our children, Arya, Gareth, and Gaia for (almost always) following the Zombie Rules.

Thanks to my collaborator Skyler Gray for the terrific experience working on this together.

Thanks to my great friend Rebecca Stallbaumer for going "full German" on the manuscript.

Capability Sets by Career

Architect

Adobe InDesign

Advanced mathematics

AIA membership

Analysis

AutoCAD

AutoDesk 3d Max

Building information modeling (BIM)

Change orders

Client presentation

Communication skills

Construction processes

Knowledge of architectural history

Leadership

Problem solving

Project management

Revit

Request for information (RFI)

Request for proposal (RFP)

Site visits

SketchUp

Teamwork

Eldercare Nurse

Advanced cardiac life support (ACLS)

Basic life support (BLS)

Cardiopulmonary resuscitation (CPR)

Communication

Compassion

Critical care medicine

Fiscal management

Geriatrics

Home care

Initiative

Interpersonal skills

Market planning

Medication administration

Network contracting

Nursing education

Nursing process

Organization

Physical strength & stamina

Program planning

Quality control

Time management

HVAC Tech

Attention to detail

Commercial construction

Computer skills

Critical thinking

Customer service

Ductwork

Effective communication

Elevations

EPA

Gauges

Hand and power tool experience

Heavy equipment

Mechanical skills

Microsoft Teams

Preventive maintenance

Problem solving

Reading blueprints

Shooting video

Systems analysis

Time management

Troubleshooting

Digital Marketer

Administration

Adobe Premiere Pro

Advertising

Apple Final Cut Pro

Campaigns

Communication

Computer literacy

Content management systems (CMS)

Content marketing

Data analytics

Design thinking

Editing

Google Analytics

Marketing campaign management

Microsoft Excel

Microsoft Office

Microsoft Outlook

Microsoft PowerPoint

Persuasion

RFI

Search engine marketing (SEM)

Search engine optimization (SEO)

Video marketing

Writing

Sports Photographer

A creative mind

A dynamic photographic portfolio

Ability to work to deadlines

Adobe Lightroom

Adobe Photoshop

An eye for detail, shape, color, and form

Attention to detail

Commercial photography

Creative direction

Editorial

Event photography

Image editing

Knowledge of photography techniques

Libel

Lighting, positioning, and camera technique

Organization skills

Photo editing expertise

Procedural programming

Shooting video

Up to date with changing technology

Use of a wide range of cameras and lenses

Video editing

Green Tech Engineer

Analytical skills

Building design

Communication

Construction processes

Controlled impedance

Design thinking

Electrical engineering

Failure analysis

Green building

Leadership in Energy and Environmental Design (LEED)

Mixed-signal integrated circuits

Oral communication

Policy planning

Product testing

Project management

Relationship building

Reliability

Revit

Root cause analysis

Sustainability

Sustainable architecture

Sustainable design

Technical analysis

Test engineering

APPENDIX B:

Suggested Reading

Bronson, Po. *What Should I Do with My Life? The True Story of People Who Answered the Ultimate Question.* New York: Random House, 2002.

Burnett, Bill and Dave Evans. *Designing Your Life: How to Build a Well-Lived, Joyful Life.* New York: Knopf, 2016.

Burns, David. *Feeling Good: The New Mood Therapy.* New York: William Morrow, 1999.

Carnegie, Dale. *How to Win Friends and Influence People.* New York: Simon & Schuster, 1936.

Chamine, Shirzad. *Positive Intelligence: Why Only 20% of Teams and Individuals Achieve Their True Potential and How You Can Achieve Yours.* Austin, Texas: Greenleaf Book Group Press, 2012.

Coelho, Paulo. *The Alchemist: A Fable About Following Your Dream.* New York: HarperCollins, 1993.

Damon, William. *The Path to Purpose: How Young People Find Their Calling in Life*. New York: Free Press, 2008.

Dorsey, Jared and Denise Villa. *Zconomy: How Gen Z Will Change the Future of Business—and What to Do About It*. New York: Harper Business, 2020.

Duckworth, Angela. *Grit: The Power of Passion and Perseverance*. New York: Scribner, 2016.

Dweck, Carol. *Mindset: The New Psychology of Success*. New York: Random House, 2006.

Frankl, Victor E. *Man's Search for Meaning: The Classic Tribute to Hope from the Holocaust*. Boston: Beacon Press, 2006.

Galloway, Scott. *Adrift: America in 100 Charts*. New York: Portfolio, 2022.

Galloway, Scott. *The Algebra of Happiness: Notes on the Pursuit of Success, Love, and Meaning*. New York: Portfolio, 2019.

García, Héctor and Francesc Miralles. *Ikigai: The Japanese Secret to a Long and Happy Life*. New York: Penguin Life, 2017.

Godin, Seth. *The Dip: A Little Book That Teaches You When to Quit (and When to Stick)*. New York: Portfolio, 2018.

Kalleberg, Arne L. *Precarious Lives: Job Insecurity and Well-Being in Rich Democracies*. Cambridge, UK: Polity Press, 2018.

Lukianoff, Greg and Jonathan Haidt. *The Coddling of the American Mind: How Good Intentions and Bad Ideas Are Setting Up a Generation for Failure*. New York: Penguin Press, 2018.

McConaughey, Matthew. *Greenlights*. New York: Crown, 2020.

Wenner Moyer, Melinda. *How to Raise Kids Who Aren't Assholes: Science-Based Strategies for Better Parenting—from Tots to Teens*. New York: G.P. Putnam's Sons, 2021.

Notes

Dedication

1. William Damon, *The Path to Purpose: Helping Our Children Find Their Calling in Life* (New York: Free Press, 2008), 60.

Introduction

1. "Leading Causes of Death," Centers for Disease Control and Prevention, accessed January 18, 2023, https://www.cdc.gov/nchs/fastats/leading-causes-of-death.htm; John J. Ratey, "Can Exercise Help Treat Anxiety?" Harvard Health, October 2019, https://www.health.harvard.edu/blog/can-exercise-help-treat-anxiety-2019102418096.

2. Jason Dorsey and Denise Villa, *Zconomy: How Gen Z Will Change the Future of Business—and What to Do About It* (New York: Harper Business, 2020).

Chapter 1

1. William Damon, *The Path to Purpose: Helping Our Children Find Their Calling in Life* (New York: Free Press, 2008), 60.

2. Barrett Wissman, "An Accountability Partner Makes You Vastly More Likely to Succeed," *Entrepreneur*, March 2018, https://www.entrepreneur.com/leadership/an-accountability-partner-makes-you-vastly-more-likely-to/310062.

Chapter 2

1. The Harvard Study of Adult Development website, www.adultdevelopmentstudy.org.

2. Mark Manson, "7 Strange Questions That Help You Find Your Life Purpose," *Mark Manson* (blog), December 30, 2020, https://markmanson.net/life-purpose.

3. William Damon, *The Path to Purpose: Helping Our Children Find Their Calling in Life* (New York: Free Press, 2008).

4. Melinda Wenner Moyer, *How to Raise Kids Who Aren't Assholes: Science-Based Strategies for Better Parenting—from Tots to Teens* (New York: G.P. Putnam's Sons, 2021).

5. Damon, *The Path to Purpose*.

6. Paulo Coelho, *The Alchemist: A Fable About Following Your Dream* (New York: HarperCollins, 1993).

7. Kerri Lee Alexander, "Ruth Bader Ginsburg," National Women's History Museum, https://www.womenshistory.org/education-resources/biographies/ruth-bader-ginsburg.

Chapter 3

1. Mauro V. Mendlowicz, Michelle N. Levitan, Antonio E. Nardi, and Edward Shorter, "The Notable Humanist and Scientist Aaron Beck

(1921–2021), the Revolutionary Founder of Cognitive Therapy," *The Brazilian Journal of Psychology* 44, no. 3 (March 14, 2022), https://doi.org/10.1590/1516-4446-2021-2409.

2. Greg Lukianoff and Jonathan Haidt, *The Coddling of the American Mind: How Good Intentions and Bad Ideas Are Setting Up a Generation for Failure* (New York: Penguin Press, 2018).

3. Angela Duckworth, *Grit: The Power of Passion and Perseverance* (New York: Scribner, 2016).

4. Viktor E. Frankl, *Man's Search for Meaning: The Classic Tribute to Hope from the Holocaust* (Boston: Beacon Press, 2006). Frankl's account: "Everything can be taken from a man but one thing: the last of the human freedoms—to choose one's attitude in any given set of circumstances, to choose one's own way. . . . A decision which determined whether you would or would not submit to those powers which threatened to rob you of your very self, your inner freedom."

Chapter 4

1. David Burns, *Feeling Good: The New Mood Therapy* (New York: William Morrow, 1999).

Chapter 5

1. Angela Duckworth, *Grit: The Power of Passion and Perseverance* (New York: Scribner, 2016), 97–98.

2. Duckworth, *Grit*, 149–150.

3. Mark Manson, "7 Strange Questions That Help You Find Your Life Purpose," *Mark Manson* (blog), December 30, 2020, https://markmanson.net/life-purpose.

4. Duckworth, *Grit*, 103.

Chapter 6

1. Bill Burnett and Dave Evans, *Designing Your Life: How to Build a Well-Lived, Joyful Life* (New York: Knopf, 2016).

2. Carol S. Dweck, *Mindset: The New Psychology of Success* (New York: Random House, 2007).

3. "The Typefinder Personality Test," Truity, https://www.truity.com/test/type-finder-personality-test-new; "Myers & Briggs' 16 Personality Types," Truity, https://www.truity.com/page/16-personality-types-myers-briggs. Once you click through to your type, you'll see tabs for an overview of the personality, its strengths, best career matches, and how it behaves in relationships with other types.

Chapter 7

1. Scott Galloway, *Adrift: America in 100 Charts* (New York: Portfolio, 2022); "Quartiles and Selected Deciles of Usual Weekly Earnings by Educational Attainment," United States Bureau of Labor Statistics, https://www.bls.gov/charts/usual-weekly-earnings/usual-weekly-earnings-by-quartiles-and-selected-deciles-by-education.htm.

2. "Was Your Degree Really Worth It?" *The Economist*, April 3, 2023, https://www.economist.com/international/2023/04/03/was-your-degree-really-worth-it.

3. Galloway, *Adrift*.

4. Dale Carnegie, *How to Win Friends and Influence People* (New York: Simon & Schuster, 1936).

Chapter 8

1. Dominic Green, "These Huge Brands' Early Websites from the 1990s Looked Terrible," Business Insider, April 23, 2013, https://www.businessinsider.com/big-brands-90s-websites-look-terrible-2013-4;

Gene Maddaus and Lawrence Yee, "Cinnabon Deletes Carrie Fisher Tweet After User Outrage," *Variety*, December 26, 2016, https://variety.com/2016/biz/news/cinnabon-carrie-fisher-tweet-1201948949/.

2. "First Complete Sequence of a Human Genome," National Institutes of Health, April 12, 2022, https://www.nih. gov/news-events/nih-research-matters/first-complete-sequence-human-genome.

3. 23andMe website, https://www.23andme.com/dna-health-ancestry/.

4. Kelly Bissell, Jacky Fox, Ryan M. LaSalle, and Paolo Dal Cin, "State of Cybersecurity Report 2021," Accenture, accessed March 31, 2023, https://www.accenture.com/content/dam/accenture/final/a-com-migration/pdf/pdf-165/accenture-state-of-cybersecurity-2021.pdf.

5. Brittany Roston, "These Injectable Nanobots Can Walk Around Inside a Human Body," SlashGear, March 8, 2019, https://www.slashgear.com/777282/these-injectable-nanobots-can-walk-around-inside-a-human-body/; Courtney Linder, "These Are the First Living Robots: Machines Made from Frog Stem Cells," *Popular Mechanics*, January 14, 2020, https://www.popularmechanics.com/technology/robots/a30514544/xenobot-programmable-organism/.

6. "Branson, Bezos and Musk—Three Space Tourism Pioneers," Reuters, July 9, 2021, https://www.reuters.com/lifestyle/science/branson-bezos-musk-three-space-tourism-pioneers-2021-07-09/.

7. "Increased Need for Mental Health Care Strains Capacity," American Psychological Association, November 15, 2022, https://www.apa.org/news/press/releases/2022/11/mental-health-care-strains.

8. "Study Reveals Lack of Access as Root Cause for Mental Health Crisis in America," National Council for Mental Wellbeing, accessed November 3, 2023, https://www.thenationalcouncil.org/news/lack-of-access-root-cause-mental-health-crisis-in-america/.

9. "Mental Health Counseling Careers," Public Health Online, accessed November 3, 2023, https://www.publichealthonline.org/mental-health-counselor-resource/.

10. Korn Ferry, *Future of Work: The Global Talent Crunch*, 2018, https://www
.kornferry.com/content/dam/kornferry/docs/pdfs/KF-Future-of-Work
-Talent-Crunch-Report.pdf.

Chapter 9

1. Daniel Kahneman and Angus Deaton, "High Income Improves
Evaluation of Life but Not Emotional Well-Being," *PNAS 107*, no.
38 (2010): 16489–16493; Matthew Killingsworth, Daniel Kahneman,
and Barbara Mellers, "Income and Emotional Well-Being: A Conflict
Resolved," *PNAS 120*, no. 10 (2023), https://doi.org/10.1073/
pnas.2208661120.

2. Ryan Holiday, *Ego Is the Enemy* (New York: Portfolio, 2016).

3. Matthew Frankel, CFP, "How to Invest in Stocks: A Beginner's Guide
to Getting Started," The Motley Fool, accessed November 3, 2023, www
.fool.com/investing/how-to-invest/stocks.

Chapter 10

1. Bill Gross, "The Single Biggest Reason Why Start-ups
Succeed," TED Talk, March 2015, https://www.ted.com/talks/
bill_gross_the_single_biggest_reason_why_start_ups_succeed.

2. Rachel Friedman, *And Then We Grew Up: On Creativity, Potential, and
the Imperfect Art of Adulthood* (New York: Penguin, 2019). Only 10
percent of the two million arts graduates in the US earn their living
primarily through their art. And what's meant by "living" here is pretty
grim. The median pay for actors is $17.49 an hour, and $20,000 a year is
the median salary for full-time writers.

Chapter 13

1. Matthew McConaughey, *Greenlights* (New York: Crown, 2020), 77.

Index

Frankl, Viktor, 59
freedom, as reason to take Money
    Path, 181
fun work, 110

G

Galloway, Scott, 83–84, 145, 150, 175
gamblers, 195–196
genetic medicine, 134–135
GeorgeAppling.com, 141–143
Ginsberg, Ruth Bader, 39–40
goals
    for Balanced Path, 209–210
    for Experiment Path, 202–204
    importance of accountability
      groups in meeting, 22
    and intentionality, 5–6
    stretch, setting, 54
Goldin, Seth, 167
good life. *See also* ideal life
    and agency, 38–40
    general discussion, 41
    overview, 27–29
    serving others in, 34–38
    standard prerequisites for, 29–35
graceful exits from jobs, 199
green tech
    capability set for, 222
    as growing field, 135
Greenlights (McConaughey), 44, 194
grit, 50, 85
Grit (Duckworth), 49, 52–54, 83, 85
growth mindset, 49–50, 53, 58, 114
The Growth Mindset (Dweck), 58

H

Haidt, Jonathan, 64
happiness. *See also* good life; ideal life
    defining, 14
    and income, 144–145
    standard prerequisites for, 29–35
Harvard Study of Adult Develop-
    ment, 30

hated jobs, avoiding, 173–174, 209
health, as prerequisite for good life, 31
help, asking for, 50
helping helpers, 35–36
helping people, 36–37
helping yourself, 38. *See also* agency
helplessness, learned, 38
Henley, William Ernest, 59
hidden costs related to pay, 126–129
highest-growing jobs, 119, 120
high-paying jobs, hidden costs of,
    126–129
Holiday, Ryan, 146
hours of work, and price of pay, 128
How to Raise Kids Who Aren't Assholes
    (Wenner Moyer), 37
How to Win Friends and Influence
    People (Carnegie), 124
hunters, 198–199
hustling, 187–188
HVAC techs, capability set for, 220
hyper-rational internal saboteur, 69

I

ideal life. *See also* good life
    general discussion, 26
    mentors, role models, and partners
      for, 21–25
    overview, 13–14
    and sense of purpose, 15–17
    taking action on, 17–21
identity, and passion, 82
Ikigai framework. *See also* passion;
      pay; strengths; world, needs of
    limitations of, 139–140
    overview, 10, 73–74
imagining ideal life, 17–18, 20
improvement, focusing on, 175
Independent Path
    avoiding hated jobs, 173–174
    cons of, 178

Thank you for choosing my book among the many options available. Your support means a lot to me.

As you reach the conclusion of this book, could I ask for a small favor? Would you be kind enough to leave a review on Amazon? Your feedback not only helps me but also supports independent authors.

Your review would be greatly appreciated. Thank you for your support.

Don't Settle!

About the Author

GEORGE APPLING is an author and entrepreneur whose extensive career spans across countries, industries, and sectors. In 2009, he dedicated his professional life to building businesses he is passionate about, including a mead-making company, a medieval festival, a summer camp, and a nonprofit equine program for first responders and veterans.

He also serves as a Vistage chair, helping CEOs and business owners experience the joy of doing what they love and succeeding. But perhaps his most significant qualification as a mentor is the fact that he loves his life, and he intentionally created it for himself.

George holds two master's degrees from Harvard and two bachelor's degrees from Texas A&M. He was a junior partner at McKinsey & Co and a lead partner at Booz & Co. He served as president of a business unit at Siemens, the COO of Brightstar, and the chairman and CEO of a billion-dollar cellphone distribution company.